Engraved Glass

International Contemporary Artists

Engraved Glass

International Contemporary Artists

MARILYN AND TOM GOODEARL

ANTIQUE COLLECTORS' CLUB

FRONTISPIECE: SUMMER '95 Tracey Sheppard. See page 173

TITLE PAGE: ISN'T MY SWEET LITTLE THING PRETTY? Christian Schmidt See page 165

Printed in England
by the Antique Collectors' Club Ltd., Woodbridge, Suffolk
on Consort Royal Satin paper
supplied by the Donside Paper Company, Aberdeen, Scotland

ANTIQUE COLLECTORS' CLUB

The Antique Collectors' Club was formed in 1966 and quickly grew to a five figure membership spread throughout the world. It publishes the only independently run monthly antiques magazine, *Antique Collecting*, which caters for those collectors who are interested in widening their knowledge of antiques, both by greater awareness of quality and by discussion of the factors which influence the price that is likely to be asked. The Antique Collectors' Club pioneered the provision of information on prices for collectors and the magazine still leads in the provision of detailed articles on a variety of subjects.

It was in response to the enormous demand for information on 'what to pay' that the price guide series was introduced in 1968 with the first edition of *The Price Guide to Antique Furniture* (completely revised 1978 and 1989), a book which broke new ground by illustrating the more common types of antique furniture, the sort that collectors could buy in shops and at auctions rather than the rare museum pieces which had previously been used (and still to a large extent are used) to make up the limited amount of illustrations in books published by commercial publishers. Many other price guides have followed, all copiously illustrated, and greatly appreciated by collectors for the valuable information they contain, quite apart from prices. The Price Guide Series heralded the publication of many standard works of reference on art and antiques. *The Dictionary of British Art* (now in six volumes), *The Pictorial Dictionary of British 19th Century Furniture Design*, *Oak Furniture* and *Early English Clocks* were followed by many deeply researched reference works such as *The Directory of Gold and Silversmiths*, providing new information. Many of these books are now accepted as the standard work of reference on their subject.

The Antique Collectors' Club has widened its list to include books on gardens and architecture. All the Club's publications are available through bookshops world wide and a full catalogue of all these titles is available free of charge from the addresses below.

Club membership, open to all collectors, costs little. Members receive free of charge *Antique Collecting*, the Club's magazine (published ten times a year), which contains well-illustrated articles dealing with the practical aspects of collecting not normally dealt with by magazines. Prices, features of value, investment potential, fakes and forgeries are all given prominence in the magazine.

Among other facilities available to members are private buying and selling facilities and the opportunity to meet other collectors at their local antique collectors' clubs. There are over eighty in Britain and more than a dozen overseas. Members may also buy the Club's publications at special pre-publication prices.

As its motto implies, the Club is an organisation designed to help collectors get the most out of their hobby: it is informal and friendly and gives enormous enjoyment to all concerned.

For Collectors — By Collectors — About Collecting

ANTIQUE COLLECTORS' CLUB
5 Church Street, Woodbridge Suffolk IP12 1DS, UK
Tel: 01394 385501 Fax: 01394 384434
or
Market Street Industrial Park Wappingers' Falls, NY 12590, USA
Tel: 914 297 0003 Fax: 914 297 0068

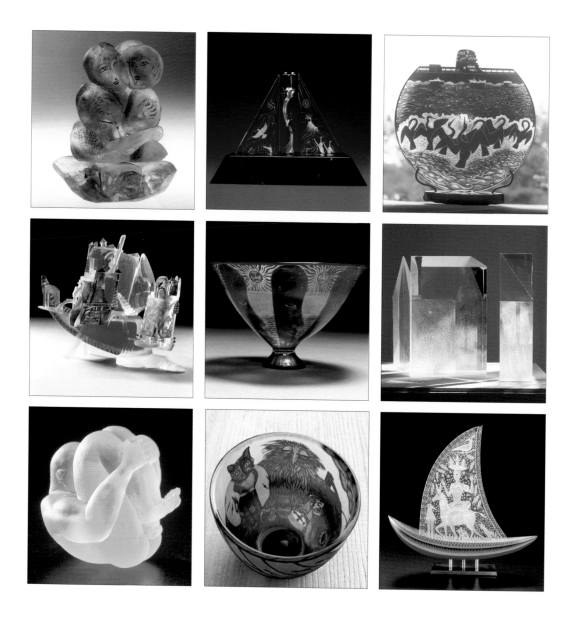

ACKNOWLEDGEMENTS

We should like first of all to thank all the featured engravers who have supplied us with photographs, biographies and information. Without them, there would have been no book. In particular, we owe thanks to Peter Dreiser, Ronald Pennell, Dan Klein, Ursula and Gernot Merker, Neil Wilkin, Barleylands Glass, The Craft Council, Broadfield House Glass Museum, Michael Nathan (President, Guild of Glass Engravers) for permission to reproduce material from the Guild of Glass Engravers, Gail Plant of the Guild for her unfailing help, Violet Wilson of the Corning Museum of Glass, and Gillian Mannings for help with the section on graal.

CONTENTS

INTRODUCTION   11

GLASSMAKING – BRIEF HISTORICAL NOTES   15

THE GUILD OF GLASS ENGRAVERS   18

TECHNIQUES OF GLASS ENGRAVING   19

THE ENGRAVINGS   23

LIST OF ENGRAVERS   197

GLOSSARY   199

BIBLIOGRAPHY   201

INDEX   203

INTRODUCTION

This book came about as a direct result of popular request – a statement which needs some expansion. Over many years, we have attended, stewarded and helped to organise countless exhibitions of engraved glass, and have been struck every time by the manner in which visitors from the general public react (as opposed to the reaction of the loyal core of devotees who habitually turn up at such events). The public's reaction, without exaggeration, is invariably one of awe, wonder, and fascination. To the lay person who has never before visited a properly displayed exhibition of engraved glass, it has many of the qualities, and much of the magic, of Christmas. To start with, the glass pieces are displayed in specially designed cases, illuminated using state-of-the-art lighting technology such as modern dichroic halogen lamps. This lighting, which produces as pure a white light as can be obtained artificially, causes each piece of glass to appear as a light source itself, while the engraved surfaces in particular strike the eye in such a way as to highlight every minute detail. Because lead crystal has a high refractive index, the prismatic effect of cut surfaces throws out rainbows. Coloured and multi-coloured glass pieces are seen in their full glory, the intensity of the light giving a unique, internal radiance to the spectral range, an effect which serves richly to demonstrate that the human eye is able to distinguish in the blink of an eye between sixteen million different colours. The overall effect (to borrow a childlike analogy) is that of entering Aladdin's cave, one full of glittering, mysterious treasure, sparkling and twinkling with invitation. That, at any rate, was how we were affected when we entered our first exhibition, and the magical sense of discovery remains with us to this day.

Once their initial reaction of wonder wears off, the next state of mind which visitors to exhibitions invariably display is one of accusation. 'Why have we not heard about engraved glass before? How long has this been going on?' ('About three thousand years', would be a dismissive, but apt response.) Then, inevitably, 'how can we find out more? What publications are available? Why is there not a greater public awareness of glass engraving – in all its forms?'

These questions are relatively simple, and this book hopes to answer some of them – except, perhaps, the last one. Until recently, glass engraving has been associated with decoration on vessels – goblets, decanters, bowls and any number of other functional table glass objects. In such instances, the object comes first, and the engraver adds the decoration, second. A finely engraved decanter, for example, looks spectacular if properly lit and displayed at a level where it can be easily seen. But fill it with port, or any other liquid for that matter, and the engraving all but vanishes. Outside the engraving and related fine art communities, there still lingers a perception that engraving on glass is essentially a secondary process – the object and its function come first, and the engraving, however elaborate and expertly executed, is a secondary addition. This perception needs to be changed, and it is with that aim in mind that this book came to be more than just a vague idea of 'doing something' to promote a heightened awareness of the spectacular works of art which are emerging from the studios of contemporary engravers.

This is not to trivialise the work being done today on vessels – far from it. Many engravers prefer to work, and choose to work, on such objects. Astonishing feats of calligraphy, for example, are performed on vessels. What emerges at the end of the engraving process, however, far transcends the vessel-plus-decoration-added-on-afterwards theme. What emerges is a work of art standing on its own. The whole has become infinitely greater than the sum of its parts. Increasingly, and in order to escape the constraints of commercially produced blanks (however good their factory pedigree and lead content), engravers are having glass blown to their own design by independent glass blowers. Inevitably, this has led to forms being blown which have no 'purpose' other than to meet the engravers' design, and thence to be engraved. These pure forms allow the engraver to escape the constraints and compromises of having to work their designs around the shape and pattern of a blank which has been blown to a pre-determined factory standard, however excellent that standard may be. Other engravers are dispensing altogether with glass blowers of either independent or commercial status – these innovators have learnt to blow, mould or kiln-form their own glass, and thus have gained complete control over the entire artistic process. Such original work is far removed from the decorated vessels which the general public can be forgiven for assuming still form the mainstream of contemporary glass engraving.

There is another reason for a lack of public awareness. Whereas exhibitions of paintings and sculpture, for example, attract wide publicity (especially if the subject matter is controversial, startling, shocking, pornographic or, as we have seen often recently, incomprehensible), exhibitions of engraved glass do not attract widespread media interest. This is simply explained. The media does not go out of its way to seek and review what it perceives as exhibitions of an unfamiliar artistic medium which has limited appeal to the general public. It waits for the publicity machine attached to any exhibition or show to hand it a package, complete with advertising campaigns, press conferences, TV and radio interviews, pictures, storylines, gossip, scandal, biographies and (preferably) conflict, the latter customarily taking the form of howls of protest from campaigners opposed to controversial, startling, shocking, pornographic or incomprehensible art in whatever form. Such professional publicity campaigns require professional public relations firms to create them, and that means money. The organisers of exhibitions of engraved glass rarely, if ever, have access to such money. Sponsorship has helped in the past, and doubtless will continue to do so, but competition for sponsorship money is fierce, and a commercial sponsor, however altruistic, usually seeks a return in one form or another.

Another form of publicity exists, however, and you are holding it in your hands at this very minute. We came to the conclusion that the best means of achieving a greater awareness of engraved glass would be to select some of the finest examples in the world today and put them into a book.

Our sights are set at those would-be enthusiasts referred to earlier, who have attended exhibitions and would like to know more of the world of glass engraving. Thus this book is not a history of engraving (though a brief history of glass is provided), neither is it a comprehensive reference book nor technical manual for students or working engravers. These categories have already been successfully undertaken, and a short list of books for further reading is provided for those whose appetites have been suitably whetted. The 'techniques' section gives a short description of each of the engraving techniques utilised by the artists featured, but these descriptions are intended purely to give the lay reader sufficient information to make sense of the text accompanying the illustrations. To describe such techniques in detail would fill an entire book and, as stated above, such books have already been written.

It should be made clear that this book is not, nor does it set out to be, an encyclopaedia of the world's most talented glass engravers. What we have sought to do is bring together a collection by glass artists from around the world whose work illustrates the immense diversity of styles, techniques and imaginative force which characterise contemporary glass engraving. The purpose is to excite, astonish and (we hope) to kindle a greater interest and lasting enthusiasm in those who may previously have been unaware of the amazing variety of output from today's glass artists.

To a certain extent, and for reasons of space, our selection has been forced to be arbitrary, and we apologise to engravers who would have wished to see their work included, and to those authorities on contemporary glass who might judge that some eminent artists are noticeable by their absence. To be fair, strenuous, exhaustive efforts were made to track down all those artists who we felt should not be omitted. If their work is not present it indicates only that we failed, after repeated attempts by the most modern – and some of the most ancient – means of communication, to elicit any response from them.

When artists provided us with photographs, they were asked also to provide a description of the engraving technique(s) employed on each piece, and if they felt so inclined, a summary of their artistic motivation, and what the inspiration was for the particular piece illustrated. Some wrote fulsomely, others a bare minimum. Strong cases have been made against the over-analysis of artistic inspiration, and there are artists who admit that they do not fully understand how the process works for themselves. Indeed some are fearful that any attempt to delve into their subconsciousness to explore and analyse the inner workings of their creativity would destroy its essence. Therefore, some of the descriptions of the illustrations are enigmatically brief, others are lengthy and lucid, others are lengthy but still enigmatic. For this we make no apology. The vast majority of the text accompanying the illustrations was provided by the artists themselves, and we feel that no additional comment or explanation is either necessary or justifiable. Where the text is enclosed in quotation marks, it indicates that you are reading the artist's own words, edited or altered only where a translation into English has become confused.

Now we need to define – quickly, for the issue can be contentious – what we mean by 'engraved' glass. Luckily, the *Oxford English Dictionary* supplies our definition with sufficient precision. The term 'luckily' is used with good reason, for it has sometimes been contended that a process such as sandblasting, for example, cannot possibly be counted as engraving. This distinction arises because such a technique has been adapted from an industrial process, and so therefore is one which no true artist would contemplate using – or so the reasoning used to run. Nowadays, more liberal views prevail, and so the *OED*'s definition, 'to cut into (a hard material)...to carve (an inscription, figures, etc.) upon a surface' is the one which has been adopted as the criterion in this book. It is also worth noting that, almost from its inception, the Guild of Glass Engravers (q.v.) has listed both sandblasting and acid etching as legitimate forms of engraving.

Our enthusiasm for engraved glass was first fired, like that of so many other devotees, by the books of Laurence Whistler. If we can kindle even a fraction of that enthusiasm for the work of today's engravers, within a new audience, this book will have achieved its purpose.

Tom and Marilyn Goodearl
Dartmouth 1998

GLASSMAKING –
BRIEF HISTORICAL NOTES

Writing in A.D. 30, Pliny retold the legend of how, some 2,000 years before his own time, Phoenician sailors were camping on the sandy banks of a river at Sidon in Syria. They built a hearth for their camp fire using large pieces of 'natron' (mineral sodium carbonate) taken from their cargo, and then lit the fire beneath their cooking pots to cook. On the following morning, they discovered that the incandescent sand had fused with the natron to form large chunks of a clear substance – glass.

Whether this account is true or not, glass was certainly known by the middle of the third millennium B.C., and was being produced in large quantities in Egypt to about 1500 B.C. The ingredients used were sand, calcium carbonate (limestone), native sodium carbonate, and various other minerals as colouring agents. The glass which the Egyptians made was generally opaque or opalescent, because they were unable to produce high enough temperatures to expel the gas bubbles formed inside the glass. Beads had always been popular in Egypt, either carved in precious stones or made of clay and covered with a blue glaze. Now they were able to make beads entirely of glass, and many of these have been found in the Middle East, a turquoise blue being the favourite colour. Blue vases have also survived, some beautifully decorated with threads of white or amber glass.

The art of producing glass went into decline thereafter, but was revived by the Greeks in the sixth century B.C., and from Greece it spread to the Hellenistic and Roman worlds, and Alexandria, founded in 331 B.C., emerged as an outstanding centre of manufacture. It was here that the use of opaque coloured glass in inlay, mosaic techniques, and the first wheel engraving and gilding emerged.

The art of blowing glass was discovered around the first century B.C. and is traditionally attributed to the Syrians. The Etruscans had also learnt the art, and the Romans became masters of it very quickly. It was in Rome itself that the first clear, transparent glass was produced, around the first century A.D. The most common form of Roman glassware was light, opaque glass, or transparent glass with a characteristic grey-green tint. Among the most notable technical and artistic achievements of the Romans was that of engraved glass, in which a dark ground was covered by an opaque light glass which was then cut away to produce the decoration. By the time of the Sack of Rome in 410, most of the decorative techniques we know today had been mastered. During the first four centuries A.D. great quantities of Roman glass were made throughout the empire, one of the most important centres being along the middle Rhine, near Cologne.

The end of the Roman empire saw a decline in glassmaking, but not a complete cessation. Alexandria continued its production until the tenth century, and the Syrian tradition went on until the fifteenth century. In Venice works were established in the tenth century and these progressed on to the nearby island of Murano. The skills learnt from the Romans in the Cologne region were kept alive, and from here *Waldglas* emerged: yellow or bluish-green tinted glass made not with soda but with potash, obtained from wood-ash in the Rhineland. By 1500 the Venetians had developed *cristallo* – soda glass with added extra lime from crushed marble or sea-shells, and manganese as a decolouriser. The brownish-yellow or greyish glass thus produced came close to the colourlessness of natural rock crystal.

Cristallo was of notably light weight, and could be blown very thin; carefully controlled shapes could be formed, and as it cooled slowly there was plenty of time to execute the exquisite fancy work in which the Venetians excelled. In about 1530 a new technique was evolved in Venice – that of cutting or engraving the glass with a diamond. Being thin and brittle, *cristallo* did not lend itself to copper wheel engraving, which cuts deeply into the glass; but it was eminently suitable for engraving with fine diamond tools. The *façon de Venise*, as the style came to be known, rapidly spread throughout Europe. By the sixteenth century the Germans and Bohemians were advancing rapidly in the art, while the Netherlands in the seventeenth century reached great heights of artistic sophistication at a time when Venice was temporarily slipping.

Around 1675 a major development occurred in England, when George Ravenscroft perfected the manufacture of lead crystal glass. By adding lead oxide to a lime-free potash glass, he produced a whiter, softer glass with a far greater refractive brilliance than any of its predecessors. Its softness made it ideal for engraving and cutting, and while it could not be blown as thinly as Venetian soda glass, it was highly valued both for its unadorned beauty and suitability for every technique of engraving. At about the same time, a method was developed in Bohemia which produced glass that closely resembled the purest natural quartz (or 'rock') crystal – a goal which glassmakers had striven towards for thousands of years. This potash-lime glass, in contrast to lead glass, was very hard, but it could be made thick without losing its brilliance and the Bohemian craftsmen utilised it to great effect. It is worth noting that nowadays 'full lead crystal' means that the glass contains not less than 30% lead oxide, while 'lead crystal' contains not less than 24%.

GLASSBLOWING

At first glance the interior of a glass blowing workshop seems to be one of utter chaos, overpowering heat and the random, dangerous movements of a number of people. After a short while however, it becomes clear that each person working is part of one team, is moving in one direction only, and that each stage of the glassblowing is done with almost mathematical precision and control.

The first stage is for a hollow tube, the *blowing iron*, to be dipped into the furnace hole by one of the team who collects a blob, or *gather*, of molten glass, the *metal*, on to his iron. The metal sticks to the iron easily when first pulled out of the furnace as at this point it has the consistency of treacle. The gather cools down fairly quickly and is then rolled backwards and forwards (still attached to the iron) on a polished cast iron or steel table, the *marver*, which smoothes the surface of the glass and also serves to remove any air bubbles. The gather is then ready to be blown out to the correct shape and size, rather like a child's soap bubble. The glass blower controls the size and shape of the glass by the strength and duration of his blowing, and by slowly rotating the iron as he blows. Occasionally he may marver the glass again, or let gravity do the work and let the bubble slowly lengthen on the iron as it is rotated. When the desired shape is attained, the glass is detached from the blowing iron with a sharp tap and then attached to another iron, the *punty* rod. At this point another member of the team or *chair* known as the *gaffer* takes over. He sits in the gaffer's chair, a chair with wide, solid arms on which he keeps rotating the punty rod. He has a large number of tools to hand, which he uses to trim the top of the glass, add a stem from another gather, or add a handle. To make one stemmed glass can involve as many as five or six people. Some of the newer non-table glass shapes are either blown or poured straight into a mould, usually made of graphite, but which can be made of many other different materials. There are a number of newer mechanical devices used in a modern workshop now, including a machine with rollers in which the punty rod is placed and which allows the rod to rotate slowly down to one end, then reverse direction and rotate back to the start.

The final stage of glass blowing is the finely controlled cooling, or *annealing*, of the glass. Allowing the glass to cool too rapidly produces disruptive and damaging internal stresses. The glass is put into the annealing tunnel, the *lehr*, where it passes on covered rollers down the tunnel which has an ever decreasing temperature. On smaller scales of production, a separate annealing oven with a controlled reduction of temperature is employed. The process takes at least twenty-four hours.

It used to be a recurring nightmare for engravers, having completed a difficult and time-consuming engraving, to put the piece, for example a drinking glass, aside ready for collection, and to note with horror later that the entire rim of their masterpiece had become detached completely from the main body. This is typical of a glass which has not been annealed properly.

A great number of engravers nowadays do not buy glass off the shelf, but taking (for example) the instance of cased glass (q.v.), commission a glass blower to blow their pieces to the engraver's own design, shape, size and colours.

THE GUILD OF
GLASS ENGRAVERS

The reader will note that the letters 'FGE' or 'AFGE' follow a number of the engravers' names in this book. They denote the artist to be either a Fellow or Associate Fellow of the Guild of Glass Engravers. An outline of the Guild's history and its aims is therefore appropriate, and much of the following material is taken (with their kind permission) from the Guild's own publications. It should be stressed, though, that absence of membership of the Guild does not imply that an artist featured in these pages is lacking in any quality, skill, reputation or ability to any degree. Indeed, some prefer to work outside the many art and craft organisations and societies which exist. The Guild is of British origin, and although its overseas members proliferate, it is an entirely personal decision by any glass artist in the world whether or not to apply for membership in any of the available categories.

The Guild was founded in 1975, the inspiration for its formation coming from Elly Eliades (q.v.) and Elaine Freed, who together discerned the lack of any craft society or Guild for engravers in Britain. There was no central point of reference, engravers' interests were unrepresented, and there existed no means by which engravers could exchange ideas or information. The two of them determined to bring together some of the few people who were engraving at that time to remedy this lack of any co-ordinated organisation. Laurence Whistler CBE (q.v.) became the new Guild's first President, and the late John Hutton, who engraved the windows in Coventry Cathedral, its first Vice-President. H.M. the Queen Mother is its Patron. Ten years after its foundation, there were more than seven hundred members.

The prime purpose of the Guild is to promote the highest quality of creative design and craftsmanship during a time when there has been a remarkable resurgence of interest in this form of art. The Guild's constitution also deals with the need to stimulate education and training in glass engraving. Another of the aims of the Guild is to strengthen the links with the glass industry, museums, and other bodies closely associated with the past and future of glass, its history and design. The art of the engraver, after some three thousand years of history, is resurgent, and the Guild of Glass Engravers exists to serve the glass artists and to inform and assist those who wish to commission work from members. The Guild holds an annual exhibition and publishes a quarterly newsletter.

Today, many local branches have been formed throughout the U.K., where members meet for workshops and lectures, and also organise their own exhibitions. There are four categories of membership: lay members, who may or may not engrave; those who wish may progress through assessment within the Guild to become Craft Members and then Associate Fellows; Fellowship of the Guild is by invitation from the body of Fellows.

TECHNIQUES OF GLASS ENGRAVING

i.   Etching
ii.   Flexible Drive/Drill
iii.   Graal
iv.   Point Engraving
v.   Sandblasting
vi.   Wheel Engraving

ETCHING

The process of acid etching on glass is easily described; the physical practice of it is (potentially) highly dangerous owing to the extremely toxic properties of the hydrofluoric acid employed. This method is used on cut or table glass as a final polish when the glass is placed in a wooden frame and lowered into the acid. For engravers the method is slightly different. First of all, a coating, called the 'resist', is applied to the surface of the glass. The resist can be made of wax, bitumen, or lead foil. Once this coating is hardened, the design which is to be etched is marked out by removing the resist, allowing etching paste, when it is applied, to come into direct contact with the glass. The resist can be removed using a point, scalpel, scraper or stencil knife – or any implement devised for the purpose. The etching paste, which is much less dangerous to handle than acid, is applied with a brush to the piece being worked upon. Depending on the length of time that the paste is in contact, the glass is progressively eroded where the resist has been removed, leaving a pale satin-smooth finish. Other finishes can be achieved by adding substances such as emery flour, which produces a white, matt result.

FLEXIBLE DRIVE OR DRILL

Flexible drive equipment consists of an electric motor coupled to a flexible cable, at the end of which is a handpiece into which can be fitted a great variety of abrasive burrs (see below) and wheels. The main advantage to glass engravers of this arrangement is that the hand-held tool can be brought to the piece being worked upon rather than the other way round. This is in contrast to the traditional wheel lathe, where the piece is held in the hands and offered to the fixed position tool. Smaller versions of the rotating drill (for lighter work) are also used, in which the motor is contained within the handpiece, eliminating the need for the flexible cable. Professor Wilhelm von Eiff, of the Stuttgart School of Applied Art, was the first to recognise the potential of flexible drive in the engraving of architectural glass in 1922.

Burrs come in a wide variety of shapes, sizes and profiles; diamond burrs consist of a small steel shaft, the end of which is coated with sharp diamond particles. Originally used in dental, metal and lapidary work, they have been widely adopted by glass engravers. Other burrs use carborundum or corundum as the abrasive. Similarly, abrasive wheels come in an equally wide variety, being coated with diamond grit or synthetic abrasives. Depending on the coarseness or otherwise of the abrasive, the wheels can be used for a range of purposes on glass – cutting, polishing, intaglio and sculptural work. Final polishing can be achieved using impregnated rubber or felt wheels.

GRAAL

Graal as a form of engraving is unlike any other, in that the glass object itself is blown after the engraving has been undertaken. It was a hot glass artist known as Knut Bergkuist, working for Kosta glass in 1914, who made the first attempts to seal in engraved designs by Wollman by adding a layer of clear glass on top of the engraved piece. Bergkuist then joined two Swedish glass artists (Gate and Hald) sponsored by the Orrefors company. For many years they had been searching for the perfect decorating technique on glass, but it had proved elusive. During the years of trial and error, study and failure, they started to refer to it as the holy grail – hence graal. Despite the setbacks, however, it took the 1925 Paris Exhibition by storm.

The technique is considered 'prestigious and esoteric…exotic and expensive… the ultimate decorative glass technique' (from the V. & A. catalogue *Scandinavian Glass*, J. Opie, 1991). To begin with, a bubble is blown to the approximate size of the human fist, with overlays of coloured glass added to the designers' preference. The bubble is then cracked off the iron and allowed to cool. After cooling, it is carved in cameo. It is then returned to the furnace and reheated, where more clear glass is gathered over it. It is then blown out to the required size and shape. Thus underneath the clear glass layer the engraving is trapped, its subtlety enhanced by the blowing out process. The decoration is therefore integral to the glass rather than being imposed on it.

Only a very few engravers undertake this time-consuming, difficult and complicated form of engraving. Not only is it a very expensive process requiring much skill, but it also contains an element of risk in that the end product after annealing may not turn out to be exactly what the engraver had in mind to begin with. This element of risk adds to our appreciation of what is in any event a rare and beautiful form of engraving.

POINT ENGRAVING

There are two principal types of tool for point engraving – the diamond point and the tungsten carbide point. These intensely hard, but brittle, materials are set into a holder similar to a pen or pencil. Generally, the tungsten carbide point is more widely used by engravers, for the reason that it is more adaptable, just as effective as diamond and much less expensive. It can also be shaped to any angle between 30° and 90°, whilst diamond points with an angle under 60° cannot be used practically as they can break away at the point under hard impact or rough treatment. Tungsten carbide too can break, but can be easily reshaped.

Point engraving is executed by hand (i.e. no powered equipment is employed) and is perhaps the simplest and one of the most ancient forms of engraving on glass. In line engraving, the surface of the glass is carefully scored. In stipple engraving the point is tapped upon the surface of the glass to produce a mass of tiny dots. By varying the density of the dots, the engraver can control a range of tonal effects between black – untouched glass – and white – a continuous broken surface. Where the dots are densest the engraving is crisp and pure white. The Dutch engravers of the eighteenth and nineteenth century created marvellous pictures on glass of every subject imaginable, with both line and stipple. Laurence Whistler revived the art in 1934, stimulating and inspiring a new generation of engravers.

SANDBLASTING

As with the case of acid etching, the glass has a resist applied to it first, and then the design is executed in the areas on the glass not protected by the resist. Because the process of erosion is mechanical, rather than chemical, the protective coating is usually made of self-adhesive material such as masking tape or Fablon. The stencil cut design then has a compressed air-driven blast of abrasive material directed at it, so that the glass is eroded only where it has been left unprotected. This erosion is very rapid and leaves a fine granular texture on the surface of the glass. The process requires an enclosed cabinet (with a viewing window), as well as a compressor, and the engraver controls the jet of abrasive using a gun to direct it. This in turn requires flexible protective sleeves reaching inside the cabinet so that the gun can be finely manipulated. The depth of cut and finish can be controlled by varying the coarseness of the grit, the air pressure, the distance of the gun's nozzle from the piece and the hardness of the glass.

The technique is used frequently for industrial applications, particularly for mass production on materials other than glass, and for that reason, if no other, sandblasting has not always enjoyed the unreserved approval of artists working on glass who employ the more traditional methods of engraving. However, in skilful hands, and by using multi-stage stencilling combined with the best design, very fine examples of sandblasted engraving have been produced. Exciting sculpted pieces in which deeply eroded shapes are a feature can recall the natural erosion of weathered surfaces in nature. Fine architectural designs on large flat panels have been engraved – the constraint in this instance being the specialised equipment necessary to work on such very large pieces.

WHEEL ENGRAVING

An entire book could be written on the technique and history of wheel engraving, and to attempt a short description is a difficult task. Matcham and Dreiser devote in excess of one hundred pages to the subject in their definitive work. The following description can only be a brief outline of a fascinating and highly skilled process. There can be no doubt that it is the 'classic' engraving technique, one which requires formal training and many years to master. The first and most outstanding difference between wheel engraving and any other engraving technique is that the glass object itself, which can be massive, is held up to the lathe on which the wheel is rotating in an immovable axis and plane. This is contrary to the much more obvious way of working on a surface which is taught to us from childhood – to bring the tool you are using (e.g. pencil or paintbrush) up against the paper, canvas, glass or any other surface. A crude analogy would be to imagine attempting to produce a pencil drawing, but with the pencil rigidly fixed horizontally in a vice, whilst the paper is moved against the sharpened point in order to produce the picture.

Although technological improvements in materials and manufacture have continued unabated during the long history of the lathe, which was first used in Roman times, the basic principle remains the same. The glass is held beneath the revolving wheel and is moved against it in any direction to achieve a clean and well-cut edge. Older lathes were treadle operated, modern ones are electrically driven. Traditionally, wheel engraving is performed by feeding abrasive on to a copper wheel. The mixture can be carborundum or emery powder mixed with paraffin and oil. Nowadays, synthetic and diamond wheels are readily available, but it is widely held that for the greater part of an engraver's training, the copper wheel is superior in terms of developing the vital skills of control and feel. Wheels come in a bewildering (to the layman) array of sizes, diameters, widths and profiles, all of which have their own specialised purpose and effect.

There are four basic methods of wheel engraving, although to a greater or lesser extent they can be achieved using some of the other engraving techniques listed.

1. *Intaglio.* In this method different wheels are used to cut into the glass, but to the observer the engraving appears exactly the opposite. A good example is the eye of a fish – even though the eye has been engraved as a circular depression (i.e., it is concave), even when it is viewed from either side of the glass, it will appear to protrude (i.e., be convex). The same method and effect would apply to bubbles, berries, balloons or any similar objects.

2. *Relief* engraving. The background of the subject to be engraved is ground back to allow the design itself to stand proud of the glass. The design is then itself engraved to the artist's design.

3. *Cameo* engraving. In this case the engraver starts with a glass which has been blown with more than one coloured layer. The top colour is removed (as in relief engraving) from around the main design which is left standing proud from the colour underneath. If more than one layer of colour is used, the next part of the design is cut even deeper into the glass to reveal the next colour.

4. *Cut glass.* Also dependent on the wheel are the regular, deeply cut and polished geometric patterns known as cut glass, which is characterised by the highly reflecting and refracting facets formed by intersecting cuts; although this process depends on the wheel, it is an altogether different technique.

ENGRAVINGS

KONRAD AFFOLTER (Switzerland)

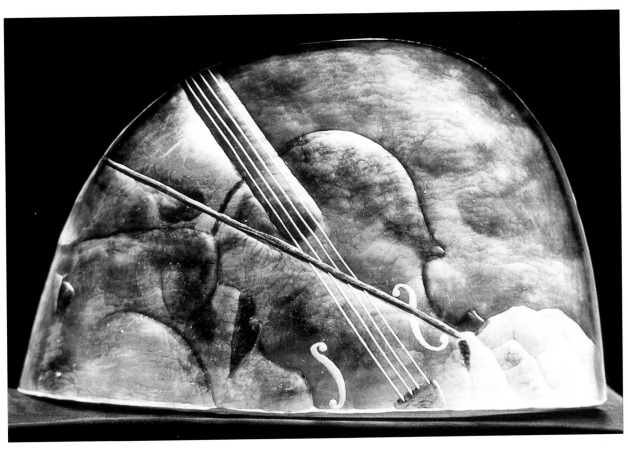

AURA 27cm (10½in.) x 17cm (6½in.)
Wheel engraved

Photograph: Manuel Ammon

'My original vessels are made of stained glass of one primary colour, on to which I then melt differently coloured pieces of glass to obtain contrasting effects. Once the pieces have cooled down to room temperature, I can start grinding motifs into the glass with water-cooled abrasive wheels. The subjects are mostly moving human figures, animals, landscapes, fantastic creatures, or abstract wave patterns which try to represent the solidified, cold glass as it was in its former liquid state.

'What has always been important to me is to make visible the distinctive characteristics of glass in its hot and liquid state; to integrate movement into this otherwise very rigid material, to let it breathe and flow. In its cold state, I achieve this through deep engraving, which forms reliefs in the glass surface. My mostly coloured studio glasses are not blown in wood or metal forms, as is usual in factories. I shape the hot glass solely with wet newspapers or wooden boards. This avoids the work acquiring a shape that is too sterile. They look more lively and individual. Melted colour particles, powder and sticks are the tools with which I attempt to make fluctuations in the linear and spatial elements.'

THREE MUSICIANS 31cm (12¼in.) dia
Wheel engraved

Konrad Affolter was born in 1952 in Laupen. He first came into contact with glass art through his friendship with the glass cutter Jakob Werner, taking his first lessons in glass cutting shortly afterwards. In Germany, England and Czechoslovakia, he was able to acquire further cutting techniques from various glass cutters.

For two of his own early works he received the third and fourth prize in the 'Central Swiss Glass Prize' international glass competition in 1980. As a result of this award he was invited by Roberto Niederer to learn the techniques of glass blowing in Hergiswil. From this time on, he blew most of his glass objects himself, refining them by grinding.

In 1987 he received a generous travel bursary for studying glass from the Commission of Applied Arts in Bern, which allowed him to visit the Pilchuck Glass School in the U.S.A. and to enrol in an engraving course held by Helmut Rotter (Germany), as well as to become acquainted with glass artists from all over Europe.

Since 1980 he has participated in over thirty glass exhibitions in Switzerland, Germany, England and in the U.S.A..

Work in Public Collections
Corning Museum of Glass; Komhaus Bern; New York Museum of Applied Arts.

FACE OF FISHES 25cm (10in.) x 15cm (6in.) dia
Wheel engraved

CHRIS AINSLIE F.G.E. (U.K.)

'Traditional grounding in drawing and design was absorbed at Wimbledon College of Art, obtaining the National Diploma in Design and specialising in stained glass and lettering. A short spell in Buckfast Abbey stained glass studios was followed by several years teaching art. The engraving bug took hold of me some years later after a chance encounter with a book on the same subject. Membership of the Guild of Glass Engravers followed with subsequent Craft status. In 1987 I was elected an Associate Fellow of the Guild. with Fellowship following in 1995. I use flexible drive engraving tools. Private commissions absorb most of my engraving time with the main emphasis on lettering. Regular exhibitions allow for more free creative figurative work. My influences have been the early Italian painters, the English figure painter Stanley Spencer and Dutch eighteenth century wheel engravers.'

SEA MUSIC 15cm (6in.) ht
Drill engraved and sandblasted

'*This is a hand made Bristol blue vase, blown to my design. The rich maritime history of Bristol inspired me to engrave this piece, symbolised in the blue of the glass itself and echoed in a loose translation of a poem by the sixteenth century Venetian poet Andrea Perugino. A sea person becomes the focal point for the beginning and end of the poem.*

'*The initial shape of the sea person was sandblasted and the remaining engraving done with flexible drive diamond burrs. Engraving on dark glass is problematic as so little light is available to illuminate the engraving. Here I have used coloured resins to infill the letter forms. The figure is finished in silver and gilt, with varying numbers of metallic layers being used to achieve different depths.*

THE VOYAGE 30cm (12in) dia
Drill engraved and sandblasted

'This is an open bowl of slightly turquoise tinted glass. The initial shapes of the mer-creature and ship were sandblasted. Fine diamond burrs and wheels were used in a flexible drive handpiece to obtain detail and definition. Both the elements were engraved on the outside of the bowl, and I added an element of colour to the engraved lettering by infilling the engraved lines with a hard colour resin. Some of the letters were gilded to give a suggestion of sixteenth century manuscript work.

'In May 1977, a full-sized replica of John Cabot's ship The Matthew set sail from Bristol to Newfoundland, re-creating the original voyage of 1597. This first voyage inspired me to work on this bowl. Excerpts from John Donne's poem The Storm curve round one side of the bowl, matching an Atlantic mer-creature as 'seen' by sixteenth century sailors. My version is based on a fifteenth century woodcut. At the centre on the underside is engraved a depiction of the original Matthew, with John Cabot well in view, looking hopefully at an early map of the world.'

BETTY BERKELEY A.F.G.E. (U.K.)

THE DEATH OF GENERAL MILLER 14.3cm (5½in.) dia
Stipple engraved

The glass in the illustration is one designed and blown in Liskeard, Cornwall, U.K., and is unique to the artist. The engraving is a pastiche on 'The Death of General Miller' and was engraved to celebrate the American Bi-Centenary. It took about five hundred hours to engrave.

A painter, especially of animals, Betty Berkeley was from her late teens equally fascinated by glass and studied it deeply. She became inspired by the seventeenth century Dutch engravers and started engraving at the very beginning of the '70s, indeed she missed being a Founder Member of the Guild of Glass Engravers by only a few days. She quickly discovered that diamond stipple was the technique which most appealed to her. She has engraved many pieces of diamond point and her work is in public and private collections in many countries. She has also worked with flexible drive and, since moving to France in 1982, she has won a number of gold medals and other prizes. In early 1990 she started hot enamelling on glass, combining the two techniques to create some remarkable effects.

PAWEL BOROWSKI (Poland)

Pawel Borowski was born in 1969 in Krosno. After completing formal education in Germany, specialising in creative design and business management, he began working with his father in Glasstudio Borowski. Numerous gallery exhibitions of Pawel's work have been held in Europe and more recently in the United States, receiving accolades and design awards. Pawel also manages the business aspects of G.S.B. (Glasstudio Borowski).

BLUE FACES 30cm (12in.) dia
Internally sandblasted

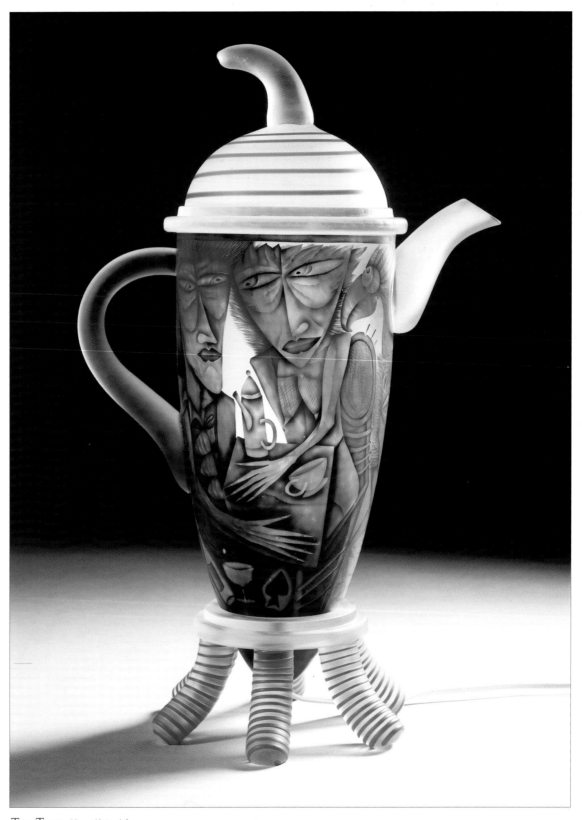

TEA TIME 60cm (24in.) ht
Sandblasted

THE BONE 43cm (17in.) ht
Internally sandblasted

STANISLAW BOROWSKI (Poland)

'A comment about my work:

'Why are people, the human race, always the main subject of my work? Because it is people's problems I depict, their pains, anxieties, hatred, agonies, frustrations and perversions; and the conditions they face in their environment of work, bureaucracies and politics, love and lust; people and everything that relates to them. But not the happy side, that would be too easy. It is the more serious side of life that I want to show, the happy side is relatively easy to see and it is shown everywhere. You can buy positive things, but nobody wants to bother with negative things in life. They are most often ignored.'

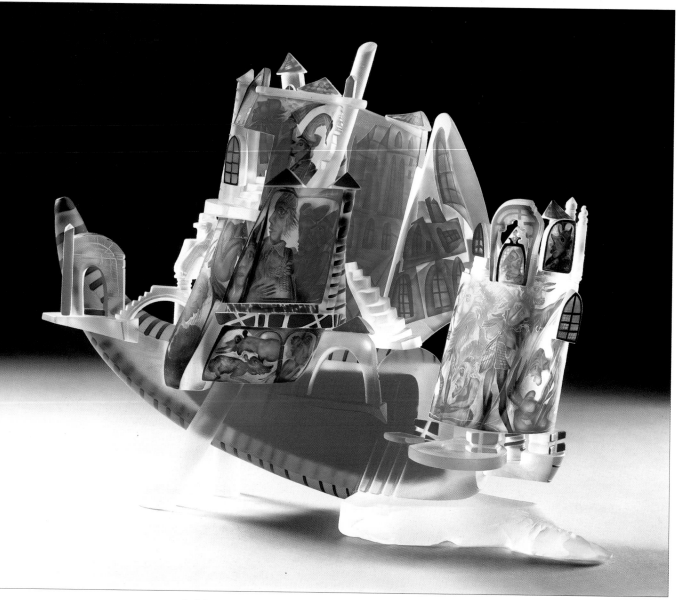

IN VENICE 35cm x 35cm (13¾in. x 13¾in.)
Multiple techniques

THE SHADOW 21.6cm x 17.8cm x 14cm (8½in. x 7in. x 5½in.)
Multiple techniques

Photo: © Compositions Gallery, San Francisco

THE SOFA   17cm x 25cm x 10cm (6¾in. x 10in. x 4in.)
Multiple techniques
Photo: © Compositions Gallery, San Francisco

Stanislaw Borowski was born in 1944 in Moutiers, France, but grew up in his native Poland. After graduating from high school in 1956, he joined the Krosno Glass Factory for formal training that covered every aspect of glass making. He soon discovered a special interest in design and engraving, with the latter giving his artistic temperament new expression. He joined the glass research department at the Breslau Art Academy for further study and became an independent glass artist in 1975. In 1982 he left Poland to settle in Germany.

His work was first introduced in Western Europe at the international Glaskunst/Glass Art '81 exhibition in Kassel, Germany. The style of the engraved pictures in the multi-layered blown glass vessels that he showed were reminiscent of Hieronymus Bosch, the finely detailed images and grotesque characters being portrayed as symbols of human anxiety and obsession. Many international exhibitions have followed and his work can be seen worldwide in major museums.

MEDUSA 17cm x 13.25cm (6¾in. x 5¼in.)
Multiple techniques

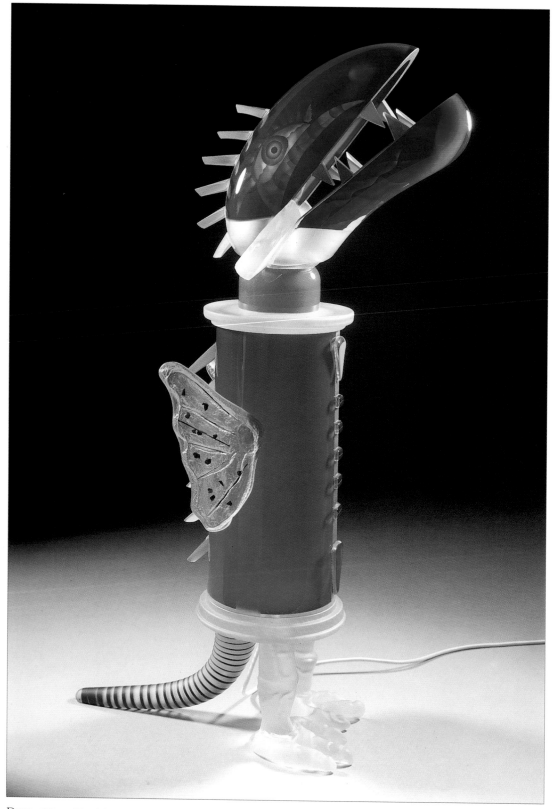

DINO 100cm (39in.) ht
Internally sandblasted

WIKTOR BOROWSKI (Poland)

Wiktor Borowski was born in Krosno, in 1971. After completing his formal education (while also following in his father's musical footsteps as a drummer), he joined his father and brother to help develop, manage and promote the new creative works being introduced by Glasstudio Borowski (G.S.B.).

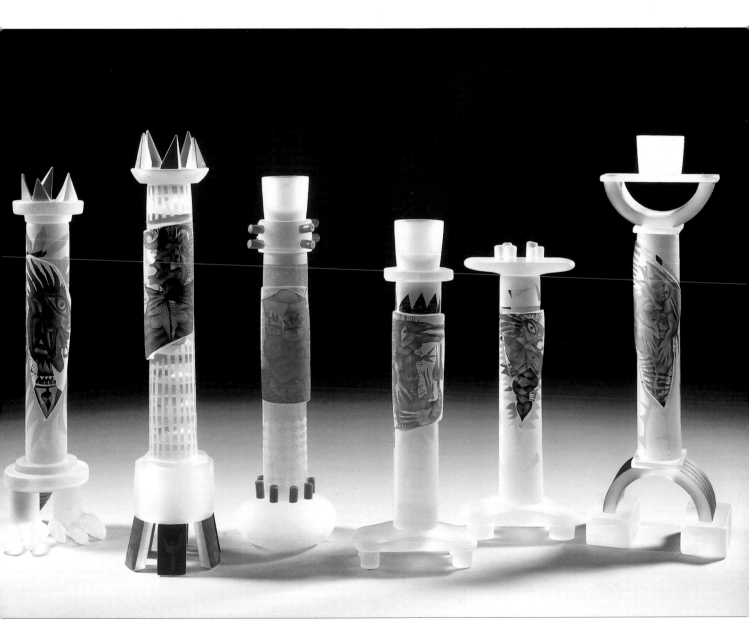

BED TIME STORIES 25cm (10in.) – 35cm (13¾in.) ht
Sandblasted

MARJORIE CAMPBELL (U.K.) (Designer)
and WILMA MACKENZIE (U.K.) (Engraver)

Marjorie Campbell: 'An early interest in glass engraving was fostered through my contact with Helen Monro Turner in the fifties, during a degree course at Edinburgh College of Art in Graphic Design and illustration. After a professional life as a teacher followed by fourteen years as a graphic designer in the Television and Graphic units of the Heriot Watt University, a chance meeting with Wilma Mackenzie through the Scottish Glass Society led to my teaming up with her in '89 as designer to her outstanding talent as a copper wheel engraver.

'This partnership (design and engraving) has strengthened gradually through joint projects and workshop/demonstrations under the auspices of The Museums of Scotland. There has been a wide variety of commissions and exhibitions worldwide.'

THE FLOWERS O' THE FOREST and THE CALLAN O' BONNY DUNDEE 16cm (6¼in.) ht
Copper wheel engraved on Dartington crystal chalice

'The goblet designs for these traditional songs are based on traditional rendering of the two motifs – the rose and the thistle. The goblet on the left (the rose) bears three roses designed and engraved in three styles – two traditional (Jacobite and Victorian), and one contemporary. Similarly, the goblet on the right (the thistle) bears three thistles designed and engraved in three styles – early Jacobite, Victorian and contemporary.

'In both goblets the music line, engraved in full, wraps itself round the bowl. In the thistle the more optimistic line rises to the rim; conversely, in the rose, a lament coils to the foot of the bowl, as do the cut roses!'

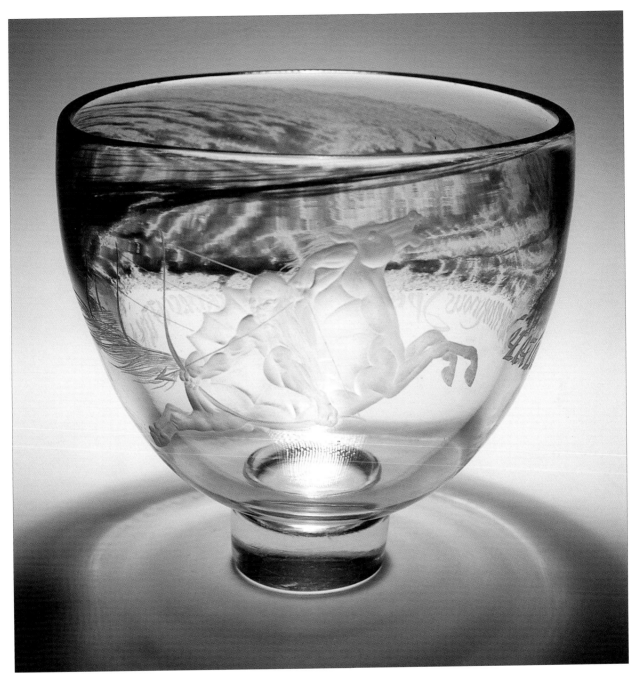

THE BLAKE BOWL 17cm (6¼in.) dia
Copper wheel engraved on glass bowl blown by Deborah Fladgate

'The piece was conceived during the Gulf War when I was appalled by the war, the methods employed by the combined U.N. forces to quell Saddam Hussein's armies and the oil fires that followed. This piece is a quotation, utilising William Blake's coded and subversive language and his apocalyptic parables or visions which fittingly express the indignation I felt at the "technocrats'" assault on nature and "the imagination". Urizen, the enemy and punisher of man, is shown on his stallion (denoting war) strafing the earth with his arrows – however, none is capable of reaching Los, the imaginative and creative force in man/woman. The smoky cloud in the glass evokes the oil fires of Kuwait.'

KATHARINE COLEMAN F.G.E. (U.K.)

Katharine Coleman was taught drill and copper wheel glass engraving by Peter Dreiser at Morley College, Lambeth from 1984-7 and continues to explore these techniques at her studio in Cheltenham, Gloucestershire. Working mainly to commission, she has work in collections in the U.K., Australia, Japan, U.S.A., Germany, Sweden and Switzerland. This work ranges in size from small items to window panels. A recent commission was a memorial vase for Her Majesty's Chapel Royal at St James's Palace. Working on either clear or colour-cased crystal (mostly blown to her design by Neil Wilkin), her subject matter ranges widely from natural history to the modern urban landscape.

She was elected a Craft Member of the Guild of Glass Engravers in 1986, the year in which she won the Worshipful Company of Glass Sellers' Trophy for Best First Time Exhibitor, and was elected an Associate Fellow of the Guild in 1987. She was elected a Fellow of the Guild of Glass Engravers in 1992.

THE OWL AND THE PUSSY CAT 14.5cm (5¾in.) dia x 10cm (4in.) ht
Wheel and drill relief engraved on a grey on orange cased crystal bowl blown by Neil Wilkin
Photo: Maggie Jenkins

'The overlay of the two colour casings produces a green shade which gave the engraver the original idea of the "pea-green" boat'.

GINKGO 32cm (12½in.) dia
Wheel and drill engraved using relief and intaglio techniques on an amber on green cased crystal disc blown by Neil Wilkin
Photo: Maggie Jenkins

'The partial amber casing in the centre of the disc allowed for the jade green border.'

JENNIFER CONWAY F.G.E. (U.K.)

THE CHILD'S GAME OF CHESS
Stipple engraved goblet

'The little chess girl is one of my nieces – Katie – she used to love playing chess and represented her junior school and county. She's grown up now and doesn't have time for such things.'

Jennifer Conway has been engraving glass since 1972. No aspect of engraving on glass had been taught at art school (Colchester, under John O'Connor, John Nash, Peter Coker, Hugh Cronyn), but she began to engrave on a small scale – stippling landscapes and architectural subjects on to crystal goblets – after seeing an exhibition of such work by Laurence Whistler in 1971.

Most of the work she does now is engraved using the technique pioneered by John Hutton (most famously in Coventry Cathedral) which she learnt at Morley College, S.E. London, with Warwick Hutton (son of John, and also a former student at Colchester) in 1975-76. She worked for a short period with John Hutton until his death in 1976.

Apart from this short spell with the Huttons, Jennifer Conway is self-taught. Laurence Whistler invited her to join the newly formed Guild of Glass Engravers in 1975, and she was elected a Fellow in 1979. She continues to exhibit regularly, mostly with the Guild, and her work can be seen in several churches around the country.

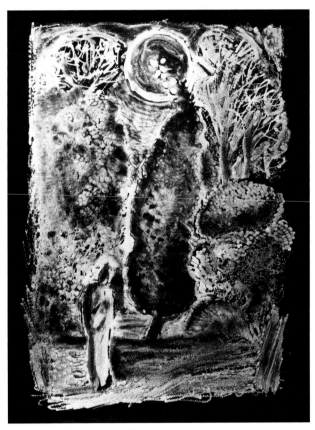

STUDY AFTER SAMUEL PALMER
Silicon carbide wheel engraved (flexible drive) on clear float glass

MOTHER AND CHILD
Silicon carbide wheel engraved (flexible drive) on clear float glass

'These are engraved using a 3in. diameter silicon carbide wheel and water, then polished up in varying degrees, according to the texture and transparency I need, with various grades of carborundum paper cut into strips and stuck on to 3in. diameter rubber wheels. I've found that ready made grit-permeated rubber wheels are not at all adequate for my needs. These silicon carbide and rubber wheels are attached to a flexible drive, which with the motor were made for me by a friend twenty years ago and they've not let me down, thank goodness. He is now a professor of oncology with probably no spare time for engineering interests!'

JOACHIME 20.3cm (8in.) x 76cm (30in.) x 104cm (41in.)
Carved wood; glass sandblasted and engraved, paint, copper

KéKé Cribbs (U.S.A.)

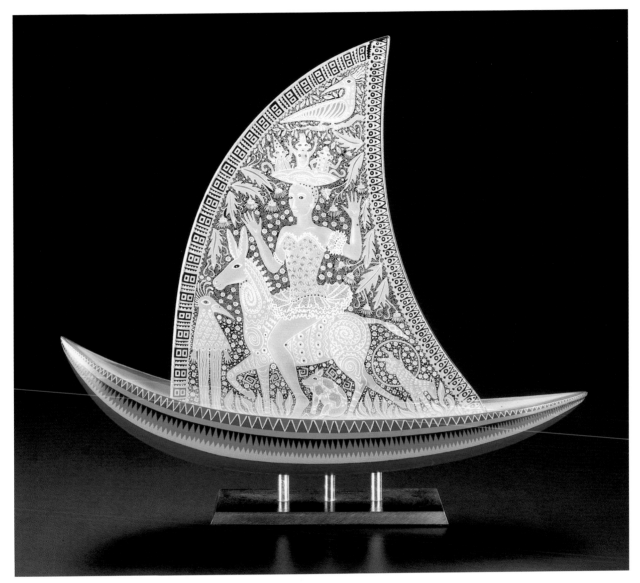

PHOEBE 10.2cm (4in.) x 58cm (23in.) x 51cm (20in.)
Sandblasted, engraved, wood, paint, steel

I began sandblasting on vessels in 1981. In 1984 I made the first boat out of papier mâché with a white on clear, sandblasted and gold leafed sail. It is now on permanent display at the L.A. County Museum in Los Angeles, California.

'In 1985, in a continued effort to incorporate simple plate glass into colourful expressive works, I started carving wood figures. The central glass panel represented a door, or window to the soul. In 1994, wishing for a larger "canvas", miniature doors became a theme. The doors with their locks and door knobs became symbols of both opportunity and memory, allowing me to delve into more personal imagery.

'The miniature doors led to a commission for a real door for Charles and Andrea Bronfman. It is intended to create a feeling of peacefulness before entering the inner sanctuary of home.'

BRONFMAN door
(detail) 69cm
(27in.) x 84cm
(33in.)
*Sandblasted, diamond
wheel engraved, reverse
paint, gold leaf*

Born in Colorado Springs, CO. Educated in Ireland, travelled in Europe and lived
in Corsica. Pilchuck Glass School, Stanwood WA, U.S.A.. Teaching positions at
Pilchuck, Swain School of Design, Southeastern Massachusetts University,
Penland School. Numerous scholarships and awards, and exhibitions.

Work in Public Collections
Albuquerque Museum, Albuquerque, NM; James Copely Library, La Jolla, CA; Corning
Museum of Glass, Corning, NY; Hokkaido Museum of Modern Art, Sapporo, Japan; Katazawa
Museum, Katazawa, Japan; Los Angeles County Museum of Art, Los Angeles, CA; Charles A.
Wustum Museum of Fine Arts, Racine, WI.

PETER DAVID F.G.E. (U.K.)

'My favourite subjects for engraving are plants, animals and landscapes. The fine details, textures and patterns found in natural objects appeal most to my imagination. I see a scene which seems to me to call out to be engraved…I photograph it and engrave it. I would like to find out why some scenes on glass have the effect of leading the spectator into the scene to

UNDER THE PIER
Stipple Engraved on Leerdam glass

THE SLAVE HOUSE
Stipple Engraved on Whitefriars Olympus Claret Glass

become part of it, whereas others singularly fail to have this effect.

'I have always engraved things to please myself, or at least, almost always, but occasionally when giving someone a glass specially I have tried to find a subject I thought would appeal to that particular recipient. I have never been able to carry out "commissions" because I find it so difficult to conceive what is wanted. The only successful ones are those when the commission is "do what you like."'

THE TROUT
Stipple Engraved on Leerdam glass

JAMES DENISON-PENDER F.G.E. (U.K.)

TURKANA WOMAN 19.5cm (7½in.) ht
Stipple Engraved on block

'I collect my subjects largely with a camera and my photographs are the raw material of my compositions. My main interests are the landscape of northern Britain and the wildlife and tribal life of Africa. I have found the paintings of J.E. Millet particularly helpful, because his combination of figures and landscape in nineteenth century France is so close to the Africa of today. I like to use a wide variety of texture in my stippling and to explore the transparency of glass by using all the surfaces.'

50

James Denison-Pender was born in London in 1942. Although drawing and painting were a major part of his life during his schooldays, he embarked on a career in the computer industry. In 1967 he first saw the work of Laurence Whistler, as a result of which, entirely self-taught, he took up engraving as a hobby. A prolonged convalescence following illness enabled him to develop his skill to a professional level and in 1972 he left the computer industry to make engraving his full-time career. He joined the newly formed Guild of Glass Engravers in 1975 and was elected a Fellow in 1980.

His commissioned works include a goblet which was presented to (then) H.R.H. the Princess of Wales on a visit to her old school, West Heath; two goblets commissioned by the U.S. Embassy in London and presented to the retiring Ambassador, Mr Charles Price, in 1989; and a goblet for Arsenal Football Club, to present to their managing director, Ken Friar, to mark his forty years with the club.

Since 1991 he has conducted several lecture/study days for the National Association of Decorative and Fine Arts Society (N.A.D.F.A.S.) in Scotland, and one for the National Arts Collection Fund in East Lothian.

He and his family lived in Cumbria from 1974 to 1993, when he moved to Scotland. He now lives and has his studio at Balerno near Edinburgh.

CORFU FARM YARD
Stipple Engraved

Peter Dreiser F.G.E. (U.K.)

Born in 1936 in Cologne, Germany, Peter Dreiser's first training, in the early '50s, was the study of wheel engraving at the State School for Art Glass (Glasfachschule) at Rheinbach, Bonn. He then worked briefly as a cutter in Cologne before arriving in England in 1955, to set up an engraving workshop at a London glass company. He worked in industry until 1970, when he became a free-lance engraver with his own specialist workshop. A Fellow of the Society of Designer-Craftsmen and of the Guild of Glass Engravers (of which he is also a founder member and Vice President), he was awarded a Crafts Council Bursary in 1977 to tour the major glass centres of Europe. His other distinctions include being a Member of the Glass Circle, a Member of the Society of Botanical Artists and Vice President of the Royal Miniature Society. He is glass engraving tutor at Morley College London, and visiting tutor at West Dean College, Sussex.

The subject matter of his engraving often reflects his deeply held environmental concerns, the chief of which are pollution and man's contamination and destruction of his own planet. He specialises in copper wheel engraving, intaglio and relief work.

Included in his many and varied commissions have been works for H.R.H. the Prince of Wales, the Bank of England, the Royal College of Physicians and the Church Commissioners. Collections of his work are to be found in the Victoria and Albert and Science Museums, London; the Fitzwilliam Museum, Cambridge; the Corning Museum of Glass, U.S.A., and numerous other museums.

WILLIAM SHAKESPEARE – THE OBSERVER 32cm (12½in.) dia
Wheel and drill engraved both sides on a single cased disc blown by Neil Wilkin. Granite base

'Shakespeare's shrewd observation of human nature is here represented by seven pairs of eyes engraved on the back of the roundel. The front shows a well-read and loved book with all its corners bent from use. The page edges radiating from the Globe Theatre have the titles of all his plays inscribed.'

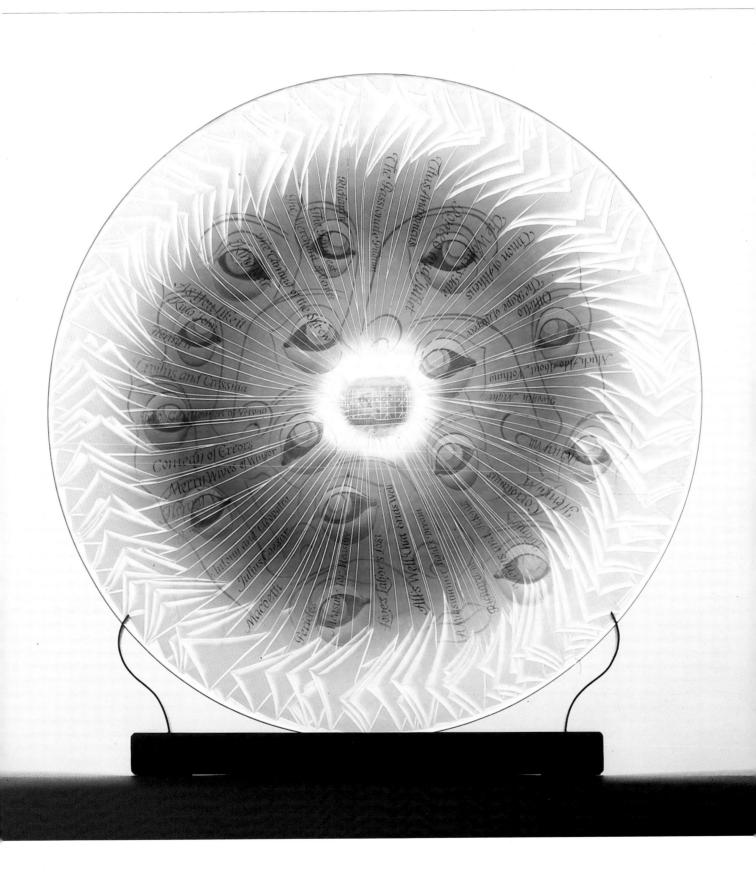

LIQUID SHROUD 30cm (12in.) dia
Wheel and drill engraved on a double cased pink and blue disc blown by Neil Wilkin. Obsidian base

'In the quest for ever increasing profits, gigantic oil tankers were built and engineering pushed to its limits. These floating reservoirs can, when poorly maintained, or in the control of an incompetent and reckless captain, become a liquid shroud for millions of birds and mammals, a disaster for all marine life.'

VORACITY 34cm (13½in.) dia
Wheel and drill engraved both sides on a single cased disc blown by Neil Wilkin. Centre cut out. Black granite base.

'As the natural resources of the western world are rapidly devoured, the insatiable appetite of the industrial monster, like a cancer, can only be satisfied by seeking out new territory.'

ANNE DYBKA F.G.E. (Australia)

BLACK AQUARIUM
Cage-cut vase. Drill engraved

'This is thick black casing over white. The thick black glass enables me to cut underneath my carving so that, except for some little [glass, left untouched] pegs attaching it, the black stands clear of the white. The shape of the vase suggested the subject.'

PINK COCKATOOS *Cameo vase, white on red. Drill engraved*

'The subject is pink cockatoos (indigenous to Australia). The white is cut back and then carved. If the white casing is even, the more the white is cut away, the more the under-colour shows through, so you not only have relief engraving, but also colour shading. The pink and white colour of these birds, together with the flora of the rain forest seemed right for this piece of glass.

'My chief inspiration is of living things. Although I've had to engrave buildings, logos, heraldry and other inanimate objects these do not have any feeling for me.'

FANFARE OF HORSES
Drill engraved

*'A vase with thin blue
flashed glass over white.
The rim is cut into
shapes of horses' heads,
and then the blue is
lightly scraped off to give
a shaded, painted effect.'*

1938-44	Working with Martin Bloch, German expressionist, London, U.K. Painting and drawing	early 1970s	Decoration designer – screenprinted glass. Hand-decorated tiles and ceramic transfers
1948-49	London Polytechnic. Graphic arts	mid-1970s	ACI Crown Crystal Glass, Sydney
1956	Migration to Australia		Glass decoration designer screen printed glass and ceramics; also glass engraving
late 1950-	National Gallery Art School, Melbourne		
early 1960s	Painting and life drawing George Bell, Melbourne, Painting and drawing	1976-78	Dybka-Tichy Studio (with Rudolph Dybka and Vladamir Tichy) Sydney. Glass Engraving, ceramic murals and tiles
mid-1960s	Guy Boyd Studios (ceramics), MelbourneMajolica Decorator – pottery decoration	1978-present	Own glass engraving studio, Argyle Arts Centre, The Rocks, Sydney
mid-1960s-	Old Chelsea Glassware, Melbourne		

58

ERWIN EISCH (GERMANY)

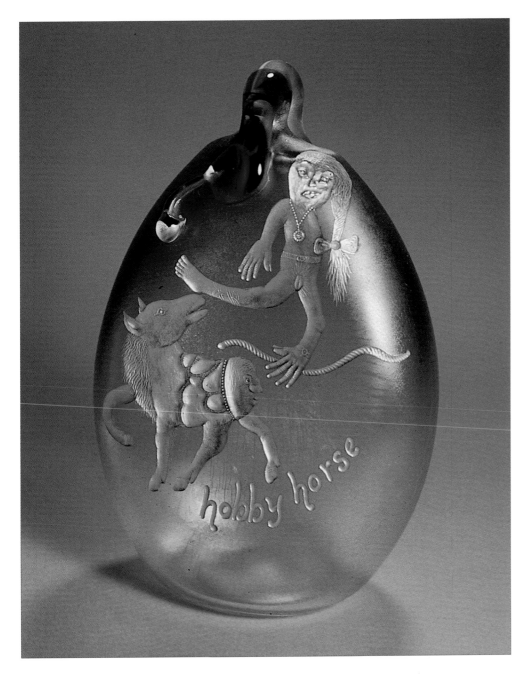

HOBBY HORSE
about 27cm (10½in.) ht

'Beauty is what we're all looking for. In my work, I insist on beauty that challenges, beauty that looks for pictures. Here I see the driving force as coming from the individuality of the artist, the root of the creative process.

'We all need our thinking, feeling and working hands as well as a philosophy based on the weakness and greatness of the human being.

'Art in the past seventy years has forgotten the body. We must go back to our real body to discover our souls, our feelings, ourselves.'

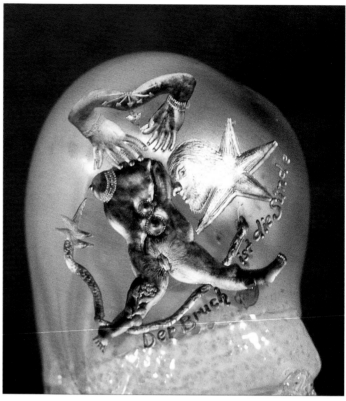

BUDDHA'S
MOTHERHOOD
5cm x 25cm (2in. x
10in.)

*All the pieces are
engraved, painted
with gold lustre, then
fired*

THE BREAK IS
THE SIN
about 35cm (13¾in.) ht

One of the original founders of the Studio Glass Movement, Erwin Eisch's work used to provoke the question, 'but is it really glass?' The reason was that no matter how one looked at his creations, they showed none of the properties with which we normally associate glass – transparency, colour, shininess. Brought up in a family business steeped in all aspects of glass-production, cutting, engraving (the Eisch family has been involved in glass making for 280 years), Eisch turned away from tradition to deny function, transparency, symmetry, grace and most of the qualities which we associate with glass.

'Free glass also means that the material needs not only to be technically perfect and clear, but also unclean, bubbly, lustrous, dirty, coloured and even opaque.' Of engraving he said: 'in diamond point or flexible shaft engraving one can fall back on oneself and realise one's inner feelings through the medium – time one doesn't have while blowing glass. It is wonderful to imprint one's wishes, one's ideas, one's fantasy into cold glass.'

Work in Public Collections
Berlin, Kunstgewerbemuseum; Coburg, Kunstsammlungen der Veste Coburg; Corning, N.Y (USA), Corning Museum of Glass; Darmstadt, Hessisches Landesmuseum; Drachselsried, Sammlung Galerie Herrmann; Düsseldorf, Kunstmuseum der Stadt; Frankfurt/M., Museum für Kunsthandwerk; Frauenau, Glasmuseum; Groningen, Groninger Museum; Hamburg, Museum für Kunst und Gewerbe; Köln, Kunstgewerbemuseum; Liège (Lüttich), Musée du Verre; Oberhausen, Schluss Oberhausen; Oldenburg, Landesmuseum; Palm Beach, Sammlung Lannan Foundation; Prague, Kunstgewerbemuseum; Regensburg, Museum der Stadt; Rotterdam, Museum Boymanns-van Beuningen; Toledo, Toledo Museum of Art; Leigh Yawkey Woodson Art Museum, WI; Washington, DC. Smithsonian Institution; Wertheim, Glasmuseum; Wien, Österreichisches Museum für angewandte Kunst; Wien, Glashaus Lobmeyr; Zürich Museum Bellerive.

ELLY STAI-ELIADES F.G.E. (Greece)

THE VOICES 8cm (3in.) dia
Drill engraved

'A crystal paperweight engraved at the bottom of the piece with carborundum and diamond wheels and burrs using the various facets to achieve the effect of multiplying shouting faces. This idea came from a strange dream.'

SPRING 18cm (7in.) ht
Drill engraved on tall crystal goblet

'Floral design. Large areas have been cut away with diamond wheels and accentuated by selective sandblasting to achieve the high relief.'

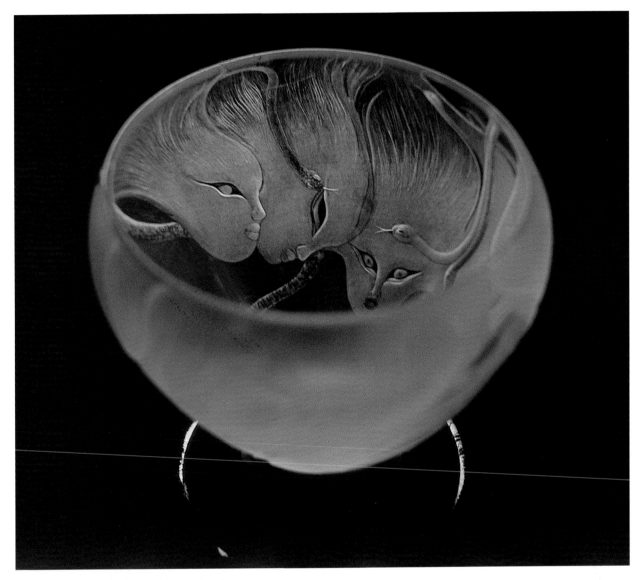

ERINYES 16.2cm (6½in.) ht x 21.8cm (8½in.) dia

'According to Greek mythology, these are wild creatures – Goddesses of the underworld. The piece was deeply cut by diamond impregnated wheels and stones and partly polished.'

'I divide my work into two parts – one, the early years, investigating techniques and mediums, with restrictions in skill and design; two, my later work – developing a personal, free style revealing the feelings and the emotions of a restless mind.'

Elly Stai-Eliades studied glass engraving and decorating at Isleworth Polytechnic and Morley College under Peter Dreiser. In 1975 with Elaine Freed she founded in London the Guild of Glass Engravers, believed to be the first in the history of the craft. She became a Fellow of the Society of Designer-Craftsmen and of the Guild of Glass Engravers, later becoming vice-president for life of the Guild.

Her work has been exhibited at numerous exhibitions in Europe, especially those of the Guild of Glass Engravers, and has appeared in numerous publications.

MAX ERLACHER (U.S.A.)

ROMANCE OF THE
ROSE
*Designed by Donald
Pollard – Engraving
design by Howard Rogers
Copper-wheel engraved
on the inside of the rose
petals. Diamond stippling
on the outside of each
petal. Engraved for
Steuben Glass – 'one of
a kind'.*

Max R. Erlacher, born 11 July 1933, learned the art of copper wheel glass engraving at the Glass Technical School in Kramsach, Tirol, Austria. After four years of training, he joined the prestigious firm of J. and L. Lobmeyr in Vienna, Austria where he took his Master Exam before the State of Austria, and at age twenty-four he earned his Master Certification. He continued to work at Lobmeyr for four more years.

He came to the United States in 1957 to work as master engraver at Steuben Glass in Corning, New York. Five years later, he became a citizen of the United States. He worked for Steuben Glass for twenty years during which time he engraved many 'one of a kind' and limited edition pieces.

Since 1977 he has been working in his own studio where in addition to intaglio engraving he has been exploring the fine art of cameo engraving. He has undertaken numerous commissions for organisations, museums, and private collectors.

CARY FERGUSON (U.S.A.)

PARALLACTIC ILLUSION 40cm (15¾in.) x 35.5cm (14in.) x 11cm (4¼in.)
Cut, wheel engraved, polished

'The main focus of my work deals with light and refraction. I mainly use optical crystal due to its purity and refractive index Having worked with glass for over twenty years I'm still fascinated by its reflective quality and unlimited capabilities – I know that I will continue to challenge myself to create works of art in glass for the remainder of my life.'

Cary Ferguson studied under Walter Langan, Master Glass Cutter for ten years. He has owned and operated Ferguson's Cut Glass Works for the last twenty years. He has written numerous articles on glass and has lectured and demonstrated in the U.S.A. and Canada. His work is displayed at (in addition to many other collections) the Corning Museum, Cleveland Museum of Art, the Toledo Museum of Glass, the Henry Ford Museum, as well as Hawaii International Airport. He has also been a contributing editor to *Professional Stained Glass Magazine*.

NEXUS *Cut, wheel engraved, polished*

RAY FLAVELL (U.K.)

FLAMBOYANCE

'The piece was inspired by the ocean and coastline, the colour referring to sea and sky. The method of construction is the same as in Greenpiece but in this case there is much more development of the edges of the flat glass with sand-blasting. Flamboyance was displayed among invited guests of honour at the Exhibition of International Contemporary Glass at the Palazzo Ducale in Venice 1996.'

SHOAL BOWL

'The pink and green inside casing forms the background to the bubble forms which develop from sandblasting after reheating and further casing. The piece is finished by cutting and polishing.

'Following the ocean theme, this was inspired by the technique developed by Edvin Öhrström at Orrefors Glasbruk in Sweden in the mid-1930s, and through further research this work encapsulates sandblasted fish forms between layers of molten glass.'

Ray Flavell is Senior Lecturer at Edinburgh College of Art/Heriot Watt University, School of Design and Applied Arts; Course Leader: Glass and Architectural Glass: Co-ordinator of Post Graduate Studies.

1964   National Diploma in Design, Wolverhampton College of Art
1965   Post Diploma in Product Design
1972   Robert Beloe Trust Award, Surrey County Education Department
       Certificate, Orrefors Glass School, Sweden
1992   Elected Fellow of Royal Society of Arts (F.R.S.A.)

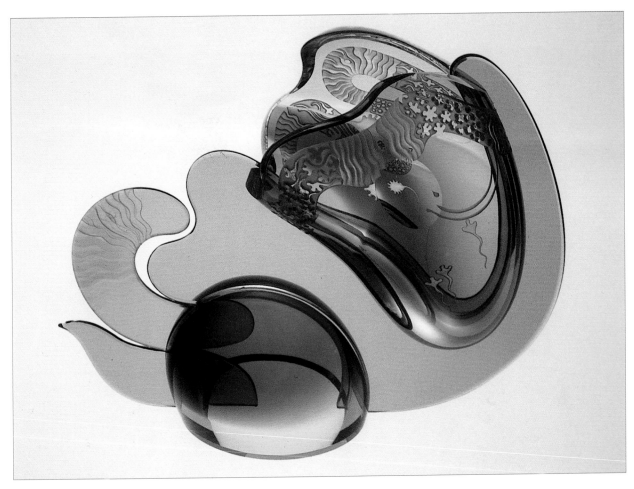

Greenpiece

'The piece is constructed with blown and flat glass elements bonded with silicone compounds. The blown elements are formed with 24% lead crystal with an inside casing of green. This has been cut and polished on the lathe, then the drawing is sand-blasted on the inside through the colour and on the outside thickness of clear crystal. The flat glass is cut to shape with a tungsten wheel glass cutter, then further worked and polished on the lathe.

'This vessel sculpture was purchased for the glass collection at the Victoria and Albert Museum in 1991 and has been on show since the opening of the new gallery in 1994. The work is a celebration of life forms in the medium of water and through its title implies the need for the preservation of the delicate balance of life threatened by human intervention.'

Work in Public Collections
Broadfield House, Kingswinford, West Midlands; Crafts Council Collection, London; Crystalex Novy Bor, Czechoslovakia; International Glass Symposium; I.G.S. Collection, Royal Ulster Museum, Belfast; Kunstsammlungen der Veste Coburg, Germany; Lincolnshire and Humberside Arts; National Museum of Art, Tokyo; Portsmouth City Museum; Royal Scottish Museum, Edinburgh; Victoria and Albert Museum, London.

Exhibitions
Contributions to group exhibitions since 1972 and has been shown in the U.S.A., Canada, Brazil, Malaysia and Japan as well as European countries

ALISON GEISSLER M.B.E., D.A. (U.K.)

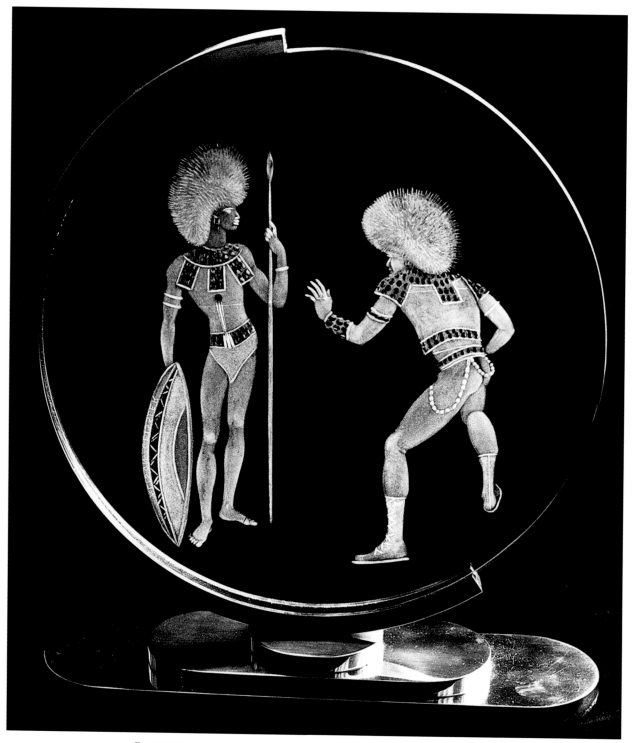

CONFRONTATION
Copper wheel engraved

'The stud design on the shoulders of 1970s youth is similar to the bead decoration of Masai warriors.'

CENTENARY CELEBRATION OF THE FORTH BRIDGE
Copper wheel engraved

Born Alison McDonald in Edinburgh in 1907, she studied design at the Edinburgh College of Art between 1925 and 1931 where she met William Geissler, lecturer in painting and anatomy, whom she married in 1931.

In 1945, with a family of school age, she wished to re-establish her career as an artist. A visit to the Edinburgh College of Art led, by chance, to the newly established Glass Design Department where she became intrigued, and then captivated, by the art of glass engraving under the enthusiastic instruction of Helen Monro.

Her supportive husband helped to install a copper wheel engraving lathe at home and she was able to practise her art without restrictions of access. In 1950 the Scottish Craft Centre opened, and this provided a showcase and outlet for her work.

Before the Coronation of the Queen in 1953 she had learned of the ten Heraldic Beasts connected with the ceremony. The High Constables and Guard of Honour of Holyrood House bought a set of heraldic wine glasses with an addition bearing their emblem and presented them to the Queen on her visit to Edinburgh. This paved the way to many important commissions.

Her work appears world-wide in many public and private collections. She was recognised for her contribution to Art in Scotland by the award of the M.B.E. in 1991.

THE LOST SATELLITE
Copper wheel engraved

'The astronauts are attempting to retrieve a lost satellite. The Earth is on the right, and above, the Milky Way.'

TONY GILLIAM F.G.E. (U.K.)

EINSTEIN BOWL
Drill engraved and sandblasted

'In this engraving of Einstein, I tried to capture the look of deep introspection, almost of sorrow, that I had seen in a particular photograph. A view of his laboratory is to one side, and a spiral galaxy on the other. The text is his famous Law of Energy, together with extracts of biography and his "letter to the nations". These were sandblasted on the inside of the bowl. The galaxy is a mixture of sandblast and drill, with the portrait entirely drill engraved.'

Tony Gilliam trained at Reigate Art School before working as an illustrator firstly in a London studio and then as a free-lance artist. He started engraving glass in 1980 using a diamond point stipple technique, and won the Worshipful Company of Glass Sellers Award in 1982. He was later elected a Fellow of the Guild of Glass Engravers.

He now uses drill, stipple and sandblast techniques for a very wide range of subjects including lettering, landscapes and portraits, as well as designs for large areas in architectural situations.

Recent commissions have been for members of royal families both at home and in the Middle East, doors for St. John's church in Hampstead, the chapel of St. Mary's Hospital, Paddington, and a screen and doors for a school in Winchester.

CWM PENNANT
Drill engraved

'The shadows cast by the disused chapel and tombstones in this peaceful and unspoilt part of North Wales inspired this engraving.'

A CELEBRATION OF SAMUEL PALMER
Drill engraved

'This nineteenth century English artist is a great favourite of mine. The engraving is from a self-portrait and I have tried to combine it with the essence of his mystical "Shoreham period" images.

'For many years I have been fascinated by the idea of linking what is seen in a person's face to what is known about their lives.

'My first engraving on this theme was of Sir Thomas More engraved on a goblet, using a stipple technique with a diamond point. But for more recent ones, including the portrait of Samuel Palmer, I have used diamond burrs in a microdrill, using a rotary action. This gives me a more direct, graphic technique, so that the preliminary balance of tones is seen more quickly, especially on the larger area of a bowl.'

Tony also runs day workshops at his home studio in Ropley. For many years he has exhibited with the Guild of Glass Engravers, and for the last seven years at 'Art in Action' in Oxfordshire.

MARILYN GOODEARL A.F.G.E. (U.K.)

PASSING IMAGES 24.4cm (9½in) x 17.8cm (7in) ht (three pieces)
Flashed glass sails, set into shaped plain glass hulls. Drill engraved

'These are images which we all see daily in our newspapers. We see so many sad or horrific images every day that I sometimes feel that we get complacent, or at least uncaring, about the true underlying tragedy.'

Marilyn Goodearl was born in London in 1936, her childhood spent in Lima, Peru. Her art career began at the Beaux Arts in Paris, followed by a course at a classic atelier. She then spent seven years working at the Art and Art Buying departments of the J. Walter Thompson company in London. In 1980 she joined the Guild of Glass Engravers as a Lay Member and was elected Craft Member in 1981. An assessment panel of Fellows of the Guild elected her an Associate Fellow in June 1995. Her work has been selected for the Guild's annual exhibitions every year since 1982 and has been exhibited at a number of prestigious private exhibitions. Examples are included in collections in England, Sweden, the U.S.A. and South America.

Her principal work now is engraved on cased glass blown to her own specification in several different coloured layers. She also cuts, fractures and intaglio engraves pieces of clear glass to form sculptural pieces. Latterly, a series of engravings on black flashed glass cut into various shapes and forms (for example, the sails of boats) has been predominant. Her artistic themes embrace a variety of subjects including mysticism and visions of disaster, especially those related to man's wilful destruction of the earth, but invariably depict the human image as long-suffering – refugee, war casualty, orphan or victim of man-made catastrophe.

REBIRTH   12.7cm (5in.) x 19.5cm (7½in.) ht
Partly cased, deeply cut and engraved, with cut and bonded central figure

'The idea for this engraving came from the piece of glass itself, which was a piece cut away from the top of a cylinder blown by Neil Wilkin. It suggested a shrieking maelstrom to me, although in this case the figure is not being pulled down into the violent waters of the maelstrom, but is being thrown up out of its terrifying depths.'

REFUGEES 2.5cm (1in.) x 5cm (2in.) x 8.9cm (3½in.)
Crystal block, drill engraved and polished

'The puppet refugees are all being manipulated by unseen hands pulling or letting go of the strings. They represent the millions of stateless people who every year are shunted from place to place with little warning and, in the end, no place to go. The mother and child puppets, in reasonable health, at the rear of the glass are left unpolished, a figure at one side is slightly polished, indicating that he is near the end. The opposite figure is polished out – his strings have been cut.'

ALASDAIR GORDON F.G.E. (Australia)

Alasdair Gordon was born in Edinburgh, Scotland in 1931. After technical school and three years in the RAF, four years at Edinburgh College of Art resulted in a Diploma in Design and Crafts, awarded in 1957. He next worked at Hadelands Glassworks, Norway, gaining experience and researching new engraving techniques with designers Willy Johannson, Severin Brorby and Arne Jon Jutrem. In 1958 he established an engraving workshop within the firm of Peter M. Kolderup, Bergen, creating unique commemorative pieces for a variety of commissions including gifts to the Norwegian Royal Family. He exhibited with the Bergen Brukskunst Forening, and travelled extensively throughout Norway, Sweden and Czechoslovakia visiting glass works and studying both modern and historical glass. He demonstrated and lectured in Western and Northern Norway, then in 1973 established an engraving studio with the Strathcarn Glass Co. in Perthshire, Scotland.

Major exhibitions of his work have been held in the Edinburgh Art Centre and regularly with the Guild of Glass Engravers, notably the Jubilee Exhibition at Sandersons and the Ashmolean Museum, Oxford, Britain's oldest museum. Substantial commissions include work for J.&B. Whisky, Teachers Whisky, The Chelsea Flower Show, the R.A.C. and the *Sunday Times*. Amongst his rare commissions was a large bowl as a gift from the Bishop of Dunkeld to His Holiness the Pope, and a presentation bowl from the electronics firm of Ferranti to Queen Elizabeth II.

In 1979 came an invitation to Perth, Western Australia, to exhibit and demonstrate glass engraving in connection with the State's 150th Anniversary celebrations, an event sponsored by the Perth City Council, Perth Building Society and T.V.W. Channel 7. In 1980 he emigrated with his family to Australia, working in studios located in the Bannister Street Craftworks, Fremantle.

In 1982, he was made a Fellow of the Guild of Glass Engravers in London.

During the period of the America's Cup Races off Fremantle, Fremantle City Council commissioned him to engrave commemorative pieces for presentation to Her Royal Highness Princess Anne, the Governor General of Australia Sir Ninian Stevens and the Prime Minister Bob Hawke.

Recently he was commissioned by the University of W.A. to design and engrave a perpetual trophy encapsulating the first micro-chip designed in W.A. for presentation to competing high schools; a sculptural example of his work entitled *Stepping Stones* is held in Murdoch University art collection.

His expertise is in demand by architects and interior designers for the decoration of plate glass for installation in buildings. Interesting examples are to be seen in Miss Mauds Restaurant in the Carillon Centre, Perth, the Orchard Hotel, Perth, and the Amber Hotel, Eucla.

FRILLED LIZARD 26cm (10¼in.) ht
Copper wheel engraved and sandblasted on Whitefriars crystal blank

DISCO DANCERS 25cm (10in.) ht
Copper wheel engraved and sculpted on Strathcarn glass vase cylinder

*'The vase was "sculpted" after a horrendous display unit collapse in the Kelvin Hall exhibition hall,
Glasgow – the overall appearance was thus improved!'*

PINK FAIRY VASE 22cm (8¾in.) ht and scent bottle
Cameo engraved – carved with copper wheels, on glass (pink cased with white) made by the artist's daughter.

'The Pink Fairy orchids are common in the south west of Australia.'

KEVIN GORDON (Australia)

Born Bergen, Norway. Moved to Perth, West Australia in 1980 with family and settled in Fremantle. In 1986 he moved to Bridgetown in the south-west and worked for Kim Pierrier (artist and sculptor) in his studio for a year before moving back to Fremantle where he trained as a glass engraver under the tuition of his parents, both qualified artists and engravers.

His father Alasdair Gordon (a Fellow of the Guild of Glass Engravers) specialised in all forms of traditional engraving techniques, including the copper wheel lathe. However, the techniques of sculptural sandblasting and polishing proved more appealing to Kevin, particularly as sandblasting gave him a greater degree of freedom when working on the larger scale pieces which were becoming more and more his speciality. By 1990 he had set up his own studio specialising in architectural engraved glass. Large commissions swiftly followed, and his work appeared in churches, private schools, large corporations such as Qantas, Government organisations such as Perth Zoo, and many hotels, bars and other public places in and around Perth as well as in many private homes.

At about the same time (1990), his sister Eileen Gordon established her own

FACE MANDALA 42cm (16½in.) x 12cm (4¾in.) ht
Platter blown by Eileen Gordon. Black flashed inside, gold topaz, green and pink outside. Sandblasted, stone wheel and polishing techniques

' – design work based on mandala theory, the design using the profile of a face starting from the centre, moving outwards in the circular shape of a platter.'

LAST LIGHT
20cm (7¾in.) x
40cm (15¾in.) ht
*Blown by Eileen Gordon
Flashed amethyst, ruby,
Gold yellow. Cased Gold
yellow, green, black.
Black lustre foot and
trail. Sandblasted,
engraved, polished*

'*Australian scene lit
by the colours of the
last light of the day,
with kangaroos and
Australian grass
trees.*'

glass blowing studio in Victoria. Her skills, gained whilst working for (amongst others) Tasmanian Glass, Isle of Wight Glass, and Okra Glass, helped her to become one of Australia's foremost glassblowers. The idea of combining the engraving workshop with the hot glass was an exciting concept, but it wasn't until the end of 1995 that Kevin established a hot and cold glass studio on the Mornington Peninsula in Victoria, together with Eileen's husband Grant Donaldson who blows many of the pieces which Kevin now engraves. His work can be found in exhibitions and collections throughout Australia and overseas.

CELESTIAL MINDS 31cm (12¼in.) x 24cm (9½in.) ht
Bowl blown by Eileen Gordon. Black flashed inside, silver-blue/silver-green outside, silver-blue foot and rim. Sandblasted, diamond burrs, stone wheel and polishing techniques

'The relationship between the universe and mind, with the light of the sun forming the curtain between.'

RISH GORDON (Australia)

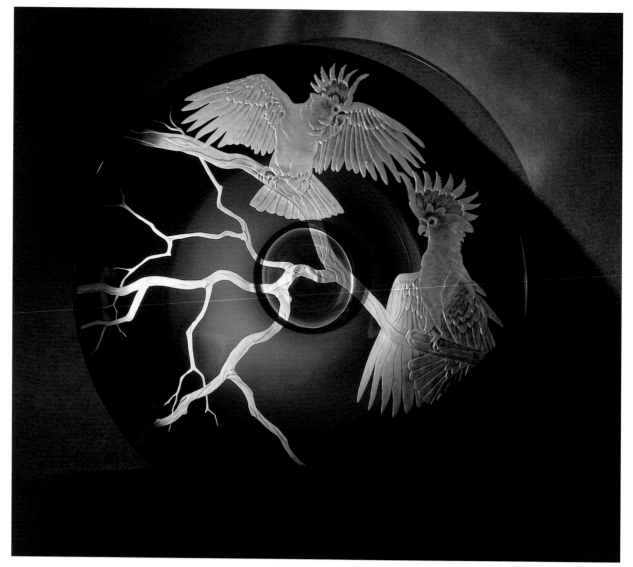

COCKATOO CONVERSATION 42.5cm (16¾in.) dia
Blown by Eileen Gordon. Sandblasted, drill engraved and polished

Born in Carlisle, England, Rish Gordon was educated at Kenya High School, Nairobi and in 1957, after completing a four year diploma course at Edinburgh College of Art under the tutelage of Helen Monro Turner, undertook engraving for Whitefriars Glass, London. She then moved to Norway in 1958, and worked with Hadelands Glassworks in the Design office, marrying Alasdair Gordon in December 1958, in Bergen.

In the same year they established an engraving workshop within the firm of Peter M. Kolderup, Bergen and Rish worked on free-lance painting and watercolour studies of the flora and fauna of Norway. In 1973, and now with four children, the family moved to Crieff, Perthshire, Scotland where Rish continued working free lance, painting birds and animals and taking part in several

DRAGONS 45cm (17¼in.) dia
Blown by Eileen Gordon. Sandblasted, drill engraved and polished

exhibitions throughout central Scotland.

In 1978 she completed a one person show in Dunblane, Stirlingshire and in 1979 took part in an exhibition at La Défense, Paris. She was also represented in the Scottish Craft Centre, Glasgow.

After emigrating to Perth, Western Australia, in 1980 they established the Gordon Studio in Fremantle's Bannister Street Craftworks Complex.

Amongst other works, Rish Gordon has engraved presentation pieces for His Royal Highness Prince Philip and Prime Minister Bob Hawke. Eight of her watercolours of Australian birds were chosen for reproduction as greeting cards by the Royal Australasian Ornithologists Union. In 1994 the Gordons established their own Gallery/Studio in Palmyra, Western Australia.

JIRÍ HARCUBA (Czech Republic)

First learnt glass engraving at the Harrach glassworks and later studied at the Novy Bor industrial glass school, and then at the Academy of Applied Arts in Prague where he studied under Karel Stipl. He has taught at Novy Bor, the Academy of Applied Arts, the Rochester Institute of Technology and the Pilchuck Glass School. His famous intaglio engraved portrait medallions first started to apear in the 1970s and are characterised by complete mastery, in terms both of technique and the capture of the spirit and personality of the sitter. His achievements place him in the pantheon of the world's finest engravers. Jirí Harcuba has exhibited his work over many years and it is to be found in most of the major worldwide collections of glass art.

1928	Born in Harrachov
1942-1945	Glass engraving apprentice in the glass foundry at Harrachov
1945-1948	Glass technical school, Novy Bor
1949-1961	Arts and Crafts High School, Prague
1971	Working as glass engraver. medallist, sculptor and teacher in the U.S.A. and Europe
1991	Rector of the High School of Applied Art, Prague

Awards

1965	1st prize, 1st Triennale of Engraved Glass, Brno
1968	1st prize, 2nd Triennale of Engraved Glass, Brno
1971	1st prize, 3rd Triennale of Engraved Glass, Brno
1988	Sanford-Saltus Award for Lifetime Achievement in the Art of Medals, American Numismatic Society, New York
1989	Prize ex aequo, II. Quadriennial of Medals, Kremnica SW
1992	Kristallnacht-Projekt, Philadelphia, U.S.A., Gold Award

FRANZ KAFKA 16cm (6¼in.) dia
Photo: Gabriel Urbánek

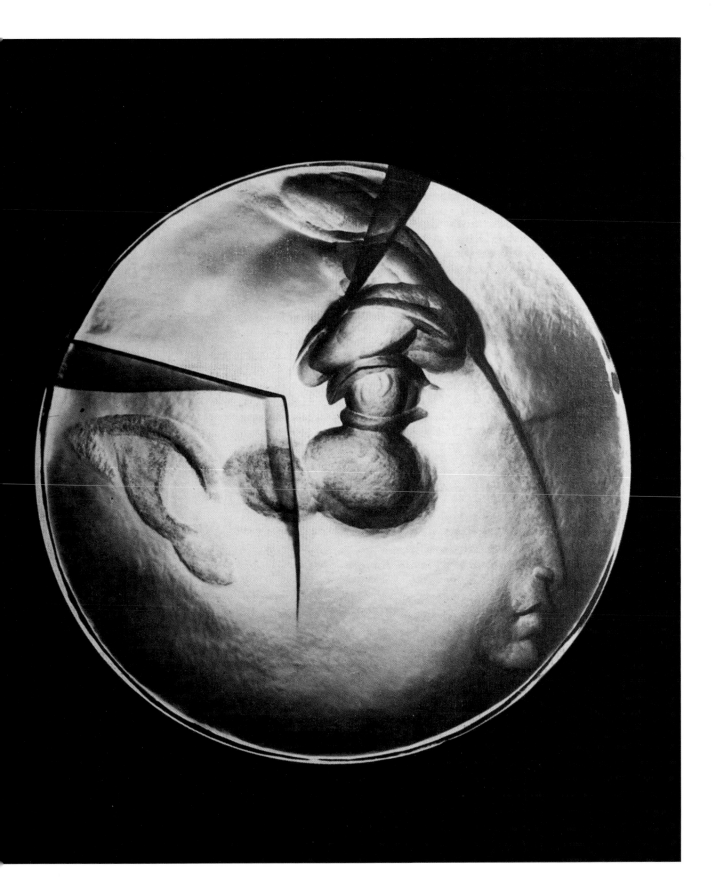

JOSEPHINE HARRIS F.G.E. (U.K.)

Josephine Harris finds inspiration in engraved glass and aims to capture mood and drama in the expression of ideas. Her work is mostly about celebration and commemoration, for patrons who commission one-off pieces. Her artistic roots are set in a much valued art school background, as a result of which, excited by the different moods of light on landscapes and buildings, she was inspired to work on two-dimensional surfaces. Discovery of the magic of glass came much later and remains an integral part of her work.

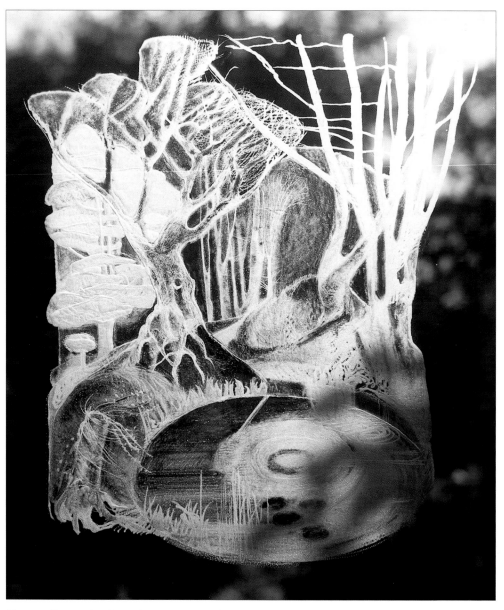

FOREST POOL 45cm (17¾in.) x 50cm (19¾in.) ht
Drill engraved on 4mm (⅛in.) float glass

'*...aims to express the silence of a newly discovered place.*'

A SPRITE WITH A SECRET
Drill engraved

'…*was inspired by the use of distortion in a mound of glass… from two view points.*'

CLARE HENSHAW M.A., R.C.A. (U.K.)

'Through mark-making and transposing drawings into glass engraving in a painterly way, my work has a predominantly narrative theme which embraces thoughts and ideas about the journey and the huge potential in all our experience.'

BRIDGIT 23cm (9in.) ht x 23cm (9in.) ht
Photo: Brian Nash

WAITING 46cm (18in.) dia
Photo: Brian Nash

THE PROCESSION 20cm (8¾in.) ht x 30cm (11¾in.) dia
Photo: Brian Nash

1982-1983	Hereford College of Art and Design Diploma in Art and Design
1984-1988	W. Surrey College of Art and Design BA (Hons) 1st. Class 3DD Glass
1985-1986	Assistant to Ida Lochen and Peter Svarrer, Copenhagen, Denmark
1988-1990	Royal College of Art MA Ceramics and Glass
1991-1992	Senior Lecturer at West Surrey College of Art and Design
1996	Glass Engraving Workshop with women from the Mutitjulu Community, Northern Territories, Australia

Clare Henshaw's work can be seen in numerous collections including: Broadfield House Glass Museum, Kingswinford; the Crafts Council Collection; Norwich Castle Museum; the Ulster Museum, Belfast, N. Ireland; the Victoria and Albert Museum, London.

FRANZ X. HÖLLER (Germany)

POLAR ORDER 34cm (13½in.) x 18cm (7in.) x 11cm (4½in.)
16cm (6¼in.) x 18cm (7in.) x 11 cm (4½in.)
Two separate parts. Dark green optical glass, engraved.

'The geometrical, the constructional, and, on the other hand, the emotional. The rational, systematic, orderly and logical faces the emotions and feelings at opposite poles. Tectonic and spatial forms belong to the geometric concept; edges, angles and surfaces of the object are in part congruent with the surrounding space, and in this way become part of it.

'It is completely opposite in the case of engravings, or relief on the surface. This belongs to the area of the personal, the codes, symbols of the soul, the unconscious and the hidden.'

'My work with glass:
At the beginning there is usually an art work – or a rough sketch of an idea. Its art lies for me in the charm of the directness and suddenness of it. Natural observations and experiences also play a role too, such as the search for the connection between light and space. This analysis is often accompanied by plastic introductory models made out of plaster, wood, clay or polystyrene. I use for the formation of my ideas transparent materials in the form of simple window glass, and also hand-blown hollow glasses, either clear or painted. The end result is either a vessel or a plastic object, the desired results being produced through sawing, grinding, engraving and even occasionally polishing.'

95

BOX
14cm (5½in.) dia x
18cm (7in.) ht

*Cut and engraved on
the inside of the box,
with applied gold leaf.
'Textures of life'*

1964-67	Apprenticeship as glass-cutter in Passau
1967-70	Skilled worker in various firms
1970- 73	Attended the National School for Glassmaking in Zwiesel
1973-78	Studied at the Academy of Fine Arts in Munich
1974	Master diploma as glass-cutter
1978-81	Free-lance work as glass designer and sculpture in Munich
1980-81	Studied glass art in Munich and Zwiesel
1981	Headed a workshop on glass-cutting and engraving at the Toledo Museum of Art in Toledo Ohio, U.S.A.
1993	Headed a workshop on glass-cutting and engraving at the institute of the Arts, National University, Canberra, Australia
since 1981	Teaching glass design at the School for Glassmaking in Zwiesel

Work in Public Collections
Badisches Landesmuseum, Karlsruhe; Corning Museum of Glass, Corning, New York, U.S.A.; Galerie für Angewandte Kunst, München; Glasmuseum Frauenau; Glasmuseum Hentrich, Düsseldorf; Kunstsammlungen Veste Coburg; Musée des Arts Décoratifs, Lausanne; Museum Bellerive, Zurich; Museum für Angewandte Kunst, Köln; Museum für Kunst und Gewerbe, Hamburg; Museum für Kunsthandwerk, Frankfurt; Stadt Weiden Glasmuseum, Theresienthal; University of Sheffield, England; Württembergisches Landesmuseum, Stuttgart.

Light-Housing 25cm (10in.) x 10cm (4in.) x 39cm (15¼in.)
10cm (4in.) x 10cm (4in.) x 39cm (15¼in.)
15cm (6in.) x 10cm (4in.) x 39cm (15¼in.)

Three separate parts, clear optical glass, sawn, ground, polished, engraved.

The object: space and light. Prismatic/crystalline forms pass on the reflecting light, either as a ray into the room or in rainbow colours on to the walls. Light is elementary. I also want to direct light into darkness, and try to overcome the division between inside and outside. The parts of the object are variable in their position and in this way new relationships result. Tower, roof and gable are architectural references. Sloping surfaces create multiple reflections. What at first perhaps seems to be flat and transparent, due to the material, gradually opens up when the object is viewed from all sides. As a certain volume is formed, virtual light contained within the material, as it were, causes imaginary inner spaces suddenly to disappear with the next step. The idea of a labyrinth and mirror cabinet, a mysterious play between appearance and reality, is apparent.

'The engravings on the surfaces as spontaneous traces, as a rough, corporeal surface structure, is meant to contrast with the calculations of optical construction and, especially, to make the surface conceivable.'

KARIN HUBERT (Germany)

HERST 50cm (19¾in.) x 80cm (31½in.) ht
Clear and coloured glass, matt engraved

Photo: Galerie Herrmann

'I do not believe that we were born with hands in order to operate machines which make mass production articles out of us. The more we are committed to perfection, repetition and quantity, the more severely are we reducing the possibilities of development, growth and evolution on an intellectual and spiritual level. But I also believe that we needed industrialisation, in order to recognise materialism as the wrong path in the search of the water of life.'

RABEN MUTTER 90cm (35½in.) x 120cm (47¼in.) ht
Clear and coloured glass, matt engraved on every side

Photo: Galerie Herrmann

GÄNSEMAGD VON GEBRÜDER GRIMM 80cm (31½in.) x 110cm (43¼in.) ht
Clear glass, matt engraved

Photo: Galerie Herrmann

ANJA ISPHORDING (Germany)

VASE 30cm (11¾in.) ht x 11cm (4¼in.) dia
Outside: sandblasted, engraved, ground, polished, enamelled
Inside: enamelled

101

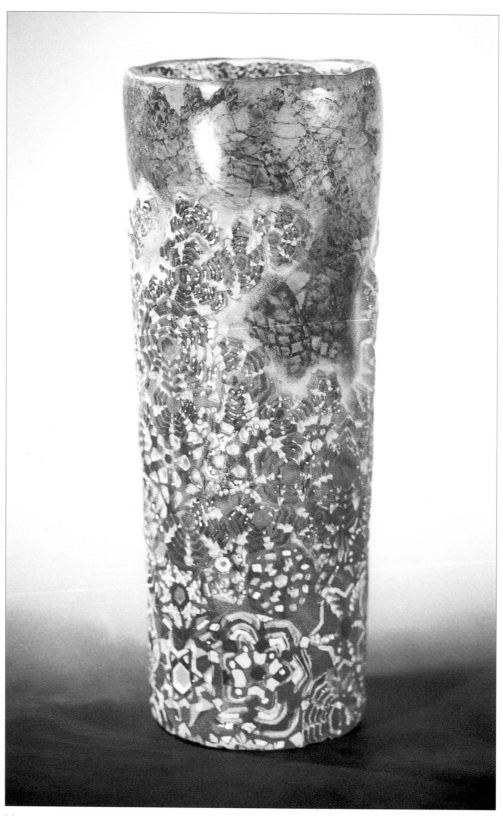

VASE 28cm (11in.) ht x 7cm (2¾in.) dia
Sandblasted, engraved, enamelled

UNTITLED 17cm (6¾in.) ht x 15cm (6in.) dia
Coloured glass, melted using the lost wax technique, ground and polished

'In my recent work, I use engraving, grinding and polishing more as a finishing technique for
my cast pieces.'

1964   Born in Hilden, Germany
1983-86   Development in glass engraving, BFS Zwiesel:
            Journeyman certificate
1986-88   Development in glass design, FS Zwiesel: Diploma
Since 1989 My own workshop
1993-94   Scholarship at the Academy of Applied Arts in Prague,
            atelier Vladimir Kopecky
1995   Scholarship at the Creative Glass Centre of America,
            Wheaton Village, U.S.A.

VLADÍMIR JELÍNEK (Czech Republic)

RIVER 22cm (8½in.) x 27cm (10½in.) x 5cm (2in.)
Glass object with hot applications, engraved

'The primary idea of my work is in a combination of classical engraving with brutal splitting, cutting, then polishing, followed by hot glass applications. My artistic intention is impressed by the optical contrasts in glass'.

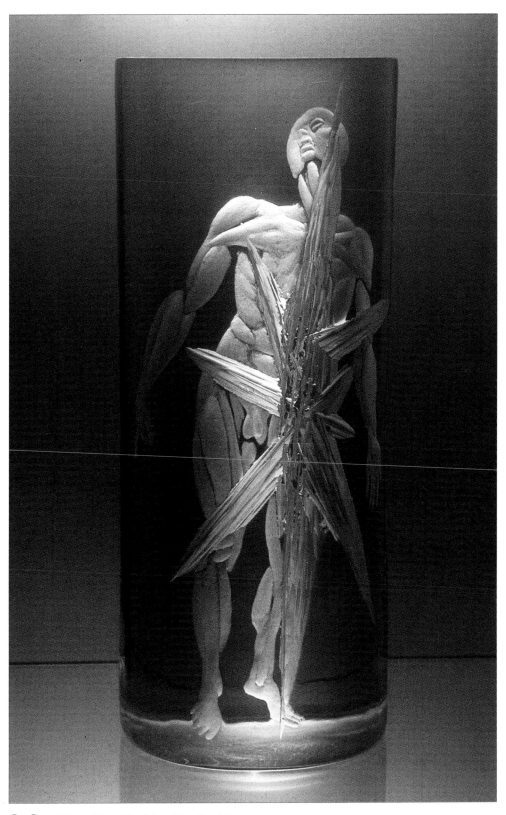

ST. SEBASTIAN 24cm (9½in.) ht x 10cm (4in.) dia
Split, cut, polished, engraved glass

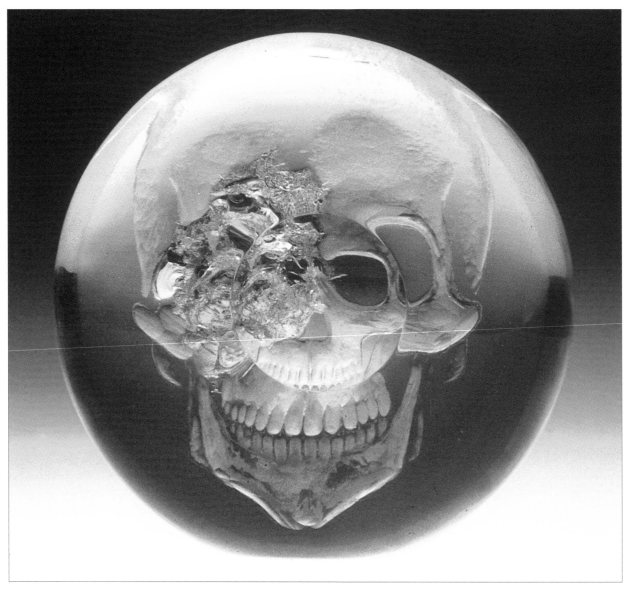

DESTRUCTION 18cm (7in.) x 18cm (7in.) x 9cm (3½in.)
Split, cut, polished, engraved glass

Vladimír Jelínek trained at the Secondary specialised school of glass making in Kamenicky Senov, and then at the Academy of Applied Arts in Prague. He has participated in a number of exhibitions and symposiums at home and abroad: EXPO Brussels and Montreal; the Metropolitan Museum of Art New York; XII Triennale Milano; Eurodomus Turin; U.N.E.S.C.O. Paris; Exhibition of Glass Kanazawa.

Works in public collections
Arts and Crafts Museum in Prague; Badisches Landesmuseum at Karlsruhe; Bellerive Museum in Zurich; Corning Museum of Glass New York; Kunstmuseum der Stadt in Düsseldorf; Landesmuseum at Kassel; Moravian Gallery in Brno; Musée des Arts Décoratifs at Paris; Musées Royaux d'Art et de Historie in Brussels; Museum für angewandte Kunst in Vienna; Museum für Kunsthandwerk at Frankfurt on the Main. Private collections in Germany, Holland, Italy, the U.S.A., Japan, Spain, Australia, Switzerland, Greece and Austria.

ALISON KINNAIRD M.B.E., F.G.E. (U.K.)

WINGED BOAT 16cm (6¼in.) x 18cm (7in.) x 9cm (3½in.)
Copper wheel engraved

Photo: Ken Smith

EDWARD LEIBOVITZ (Rumania)

BLUE PROPOSAL 33cm (13in.) x 23cm (9in.) x 3cm (1¼in.)
Carved and polished

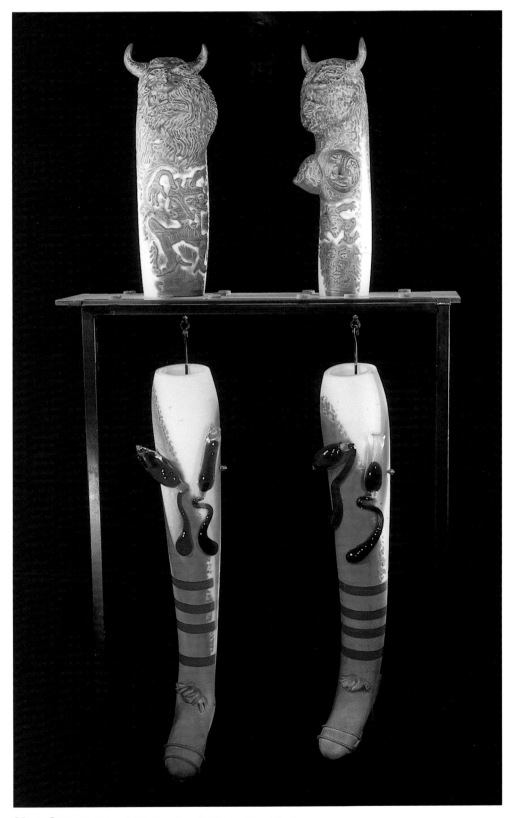

UGLY COUPLE 176cm (69¼in.) x 60cm (23½in.) x 20cm 7¼in.)
Blown, carved and polished

KOL NIDREI 50cm (19¾in.) x 28cm (11in.) x 29cm (11½in.)
Carved, sandblasted and polished

Academy of Fine Arts, Haifa, Israel; Bezalel Academy of Fine Arts, Jerusalem, Israel; Gemeentelijke Academie voor Schone Kunsten, Berchem, Belgium.

1975	Prijs voor glasraam van de burgemeester van Berchem
1977	Urkunde, Coburger Glaspreis, Coburg
1980	Prix de la Sculpture en Verre, Liège
1981	Prijs van de Provincie Antwerpen voor Beeldhouwkunst
1983	Prijs voor artistieke roeping van het Ministerie van Vlaamse Cultuur als jonge glasbeeldhouwer
1992	Golden Award presented by the American Interfaith Institute for his sculpture *Homage to Sound* dedicated to the victims of the Holocaust, Philadelphia.

Work in Public Collections
Alliance Française de Belgique, Brussels; Castle Lemberk; Collection of IIIrd Interglass Symposium Novy Bor; Corning Museum of Glass New York; Glasmuseum Ebeltoft; Glasmuseum Frauenau; Jesode-Hatora-Beth-Jacob, Antwerp; Katholieke Universiteit, Leuven; Kunstsammlungen der Veste Coburg, Coburg; Musée d'Ixelles; Musée du Verre, Charleroi; Musée du Verre (Curtius), Liège; Musée du Verre, Sârs Poteries; Musée du Verre, Valencia; Museum of Contemporary Art, Brooklyn, New York; Museum of Decorative Arts, Prague; the Owens Art Gallery, Mount Allison University, Sackville, New Brunswick; Pro Museo Judaico, Brussels; Vlaamse Gemeenschap, Brussels.

BERND LICHTENSTEIN (Germany)

SWIMMING POOL 14cm (5½in.) ht

'Optical glass block. Cut from glass cube, ground and polished. Engraved with diamond wheel, whet stone and smoothed out with grinding powder, waves engraved and polished, banisters made with diamond drill. The base is reflected at the sloping top.'

BENDED ROOM 8cm (3in.) ht

'Optical glass pyramid, cut and polished, then engraved with diamond wheel and smoothed out with grinding powder. The multi-faceted effect derives from reflections at all four sides.'

'My way of working:
I am cutting and engraving with whet-stones, diamond-wheels and also with copper-wheels used with emery and oil, a very old and difficult technical science. For this I use engraving tools with stiff or flexible shafts. My speciality is the creation of objects in clear relief showing landscapes, rooms and other scenes. I use cut and polished cubes, pyramids and prisms made of highly polished optical glass. I engrave them by using all the technical possibilities and arranging the reflections and refractions of light. Also I am working on perfume bottles and other objects by combining different kinds of glass, stained and clear, hollow and solid.'

SCENT BOTTLE 10cm (4in.) ht

'Optical glass cylinder, cut and polished; stopper in turquoise coloured glass, cut and engraved.'

Bernd Lichtenstein was born in Altlussheim, a small village in South Germany. From 1968 to 1971 he was educated at the glass technical school Hadamar/Westerwald and undertook the journeyman's examination for glass-engraver. In 1972 he was the winner of the youth handicraft competition in Hessen, and also winner of a prize in the design competition of the United stained glass factory AG Zwiesel. From 1971 to 1976 he worked full-time in glass-engraving, then from 1976 to 1978 he had professional training with trade and technical examinations in the glass technical school Hadamar.

From 1978 to 1982 he worked as foreman in glass-cutting at a glass factory, then in 1982 began his own workshop in Bremen. Since then he has exhibited at many exhibitions and sold his work all over the world, including Europe, U.S.A, and Japan.

ISABELLE LIDDLE F.G.E. (U.K.)

STORM IN A TEACUP

'One of the many delights of the English language is that there is scarcely a condition or circumstance that cannot be described, averted or exploited by application of a relevant epigram. Whole novels condensed into single sentences are made ready for use by anyone familiar with this heritage.

'In this piece my cast of players and the background sea of tea were carved from annealed cullets, using a flexible drive motor. The apostle spoon was cut from the curved bowl of a broken wine glass, as were the drops of tea which were later stained with thin enamel paint. Although the cup and saucer were blown to my instructions, I rarely make detailed preliminary drawings, preferring rather to be entertained and sustained by the intrusion of ideas from a benign source of inspiration.'

UNTO MY WIFE MY SECOND BEST BED

'I fell in love with Shakespeare when I was nine years old. Later the discovery that he had willed only his second best bed to his widow confirmed my belief that if only he had been around to see my Titania… Although further historical research has revealed her legacy to be founded on common contemporary practice, I chose to interpret the bed as my childish imagination had first seen it.'

'After being modelled in fine clay, the piece was cast. It was then undercut where necessary and its features redefined and textured using a flexible drive motor.'

Isabelle Liddle came to glass engraving via fine art, teaching and free-lance illustration. Disliking elitist artspeak and indulgent introspection, she prefers personal comment to collective message as a source of inspiration.

DENIS MANN (U.K.)

Denis Mann was born in Ballinluig, Perthshire and trained at Edinburgh College of Art with the late, respected Helen Munro Turner. Best known, perhaps, for the Mastermind Trophy for B.B.C. television, he works using copper-wheel engraving and sandblasting techniques. He also combines sculptured work (kiln-formed glass) with engraving, and currently works as a free-lance glass artist.

Special commissions: clients and recipients include amongst others: H.M. The Queen; H.M. The Queen Mother; H.R.H. Princess Alexandra; Mary Robinson (then Irish president); Compaq Computers; Roche; Mazda Cars; Woolworths; Aberdeen University; Lord Renton; the Duke of Portland; Earl of Annan; all Mastermind Trophies for B.B.C. T.V.; N.B.C. (U.S.A.); Nobel prize winner; Regeneration Award for Architecture; George Kenner Award (international award for organic chemistry); Company of the Year Award:

Private commissions have gone to many countries including the U.S.A., Argentina, Zimbabwe, Nigeria etc. as well as Europe and Great Britain.

A selection of exhibitions includes: Group exhibitions: British Contemporary Crafts, Houston, Texas; Compass Gallery, Glasgow; Contemporary Scottish Glass; Coventry Cathedral; Crafts Carousel, Kelvingrove Art Gallery and Museum, Glasgow; Edinburgh Festival: Festival of Engraved Glass, London; The Glass Gallery, Washington D.C.; Kuhler Glass Gallerie, Amsterdam; Scottish Glass Now; Three European Craftsmen; Victoria and Albert Museum.

Denis Mann is also a director of North Lands Creative Glass which has organised workshops in Caithness, led by well-known figures such as Bertel Vallien.

In 1987 the BBC made a documentary film about his work.

THE LOVERS 21.5cm (8½in.) x 26cm (10¼in.) ht
Slumped glass, then sandblasted, with colour added during the slumping and later after sandblasting

'This piece was suggested by the shape of the slumped piece. The human form has always interested me.'

ANCIENT PEOPLES 20cm (8in.) x 15.2cm (6in.) ht
Copper wheel engraved on hand blown bowl (by Adrienne McStay) with picked-up colour on clear glass
(Reproduced by kind permission of Broadfield House Museum)

'The people of ancient times; we know so little about them, what they felt, what they thought. From their artefacts we know a little but they "float", as it were, in a misty past.'

(Opposite) KELPIE 16cm (6¼in.) x 23.5cm (9¼in.) ht
Slumped glass, then sandblasted, with colour added during the slumping and later after sandblasting.

'This piece, like The Lovers, is made from fused glass pebbles. The germ of the idea began a long time ago when I observed pebbles and seaweed piled up after the winter storms on our northern beaches. (I love walking these beaches in winter when it is wild and lonely.) From this idea several pieces have grown – not trying to imitate nature, but allowing the nature of the glass and the technique (kiln-working) to have a say. The finished piece is then regarded like a wood-carver looks at a piece of wood, and the engraved subject matter springs from my environment and cultural roots – in this case, Celtic and Norse. (The name Mann has its origins in Norse names.) The water Kelpie in highland folklore lived in streams and was dangerous, causing death to the unwary by drowning – known in Gaelic as "The Water Horse".'

GILLIAN MANNINGS F.G.E. (U.K.)

Gillian Mannings' early engraving was in three-dimensional relief, using layers of colour to enhance line and tone, and to suggest emotion and mood. Some time ago she pursued the aim of controlling pieces from concept to finish by beginning to blow glass. The skills of hot and cold glass working have influenced each other and, perhaps inevitably, she is now developing the 'Graal' technique, in which the glass is engraved partway through blowing. Technically and aesthetically, her recent work reflects her belief that form of vessel and imagery contained within should be interdependent and indivisible.

Her work features in public and private collections worldwide, including those of H.M. the Queen Mother and the Victoria and Albert Museum.

CLOSED EMBRACE 45.7cm (18in.) ht
Graal technique; hot applied sandcast with metal inclusions. Blown/cast by Nordbruch and Mannings as a team.

'The face in the graal image is enclosed and invaded by hands and by the chain, web and barbed wire (threaded through a battered wedding ring) contained in the cast. The intention is to illustrate that passion becomes possession.'

FURNACE 40.5cm (16in.) ht
Graal technique, in amber, gold topaz, lemon and black. Blown out by Nordbruch and Mannings.

'One of a series depicting the effects of the industrial revolution in the Black Country (a district in U.K.'s industrial midlands) up to the present day.'

SECRETS 33cm (13in.) ht
Graal technique in blue, ruby, black and alabaster. Blown out by Afzal and Mannings.

'One of a series of three, depicting relationships.'

JAN MAREŠ (Czech Republic)

'During the last three years I have been working primarily on large-scale architectural commissions for the National Bank in Pilsen and Prague. I have also been engaged in designing a limited edition of engraved and cut pieces for the Moser Glass Factory. In 1994 my works were exhibited at Galerie L in Hamburg, the Triennial of Glass Engraving, Kamenicky Senov, and Glass Gallery, Hertogen Bosch, Holland.

'I have just completed my fourth teaching engagement at the Pilchuck School of Glass in Stanwood, Washington. In September 1996 I participated in the First International Engraving Symposium in Kamenicky Senov.'

Jan Mareš was born on 21 June 1953 at Ceská· Lípa. In the years 1968 to 1971 he learned the glass engraving craft at the Novy Bor school for apprentices of the Crystalex Branch Corporation. After gaining his qualification certificate he began to attend the secondary school of glass making at Kamenicky Senov where he completed his studies under the guidance of the academy painter Josef Kochrda in 1975. In the same year he successfully passed the entrance examination to the Academy of Applied Arts in Prague, graduating from Professor Stanislav Libensky's special glass art studio in 1981. After that he devoted his attention to free studio work. Between the years 1984 to 1989 he taught glass and stone engraving at the Academy of Applied Arts in Prague. Since 1990 he has been a free-lance artist.

He has also taught glass engraving and other techniques abroad. In 1986 he was invited to the Pilchuck Glass School in the U.S.A. as a student and then in the years 1990, 1991 and 1992 he was invited there as a teacher. In 1990 he also taught glass engraving and other glass techniques in the Centre del Vidre de Barcelona in Spain.

He has been focusing his attention recently on glass sculptures with engraved motifs inside, using the laws of optics to a maximum extent. In recent years he has been moving towards engraving cased glass. The engraving is inserted in the key place of the sculpture, thus offering a kind of glass projection. This creates an illusion of motion and internal space.

In the U.S.A. he has focused on the technique of 'graal', where the engraving in cased glass is re-heated, covered with crystal and shaped by blowing. He has done this work in co-operation with Curt Brock. He also devotes his attention to painting, drawing and particularly graphics printed from a glass sheet.

His work can be seen in collections such as the Moravian Gallery, Brno, Czech Republic, the Ministry of Culture of the Czech Republic and private collections in the U.S.A., Germany, Austria, France, Canada, Japan, Singapore and Czechoslovakia.

MARRIAGE OF HOT AND COLD 29.5cm (11½in.) ht x 15cm (6in.) dia
Graal

Photo © Gabriel Urbànek

'*This is a symbol of the creation of the graal technique. The piece was created in 1991 when I taught cold techniques in Pilchuck glass school in the U.S.A. The piece was a collaboration with Curt Brock, who blew it. It has two sides, representing a hot glass shop on one side, and a glass engraving studio on the other, with a caricature of two men in cheerful mood raising their glasses in a toast.*'

VICTORY 66cm (26in.) ht
Photo © Gabriel Urbànek

'The piece is made by laminated, cut, sandblasted and engraved techniques – it is in two parts.'

SAIL BOAT 24cm (9½in.) x 20cm (8in.) x 9cm (3½in.)
Photo © Gabriel Urbànek

'This is an example of cutting and engraving in coloured cased glass.'

URSULA MERKER (Germany)

'The topics of my engravings deal with men, women and animals, and there is quite a lot of obvious or hidden irony in my work. To withstand the troubles of this world the seriousness of humour seems to me more helpful than any lamentation. I like to show the hands and feet of humans, their faces and their activities and their relation to each other, and to animals, horses, dogs, birds and so on. Sometimes my sarcasm shows when, for example, the ladies parade in Ascot with their dressy hats, while the horses chase over the racecourse shown as fleshless skeletons, victims of pollution and environmental stress.

'My vessels, bowls, pots, and plates are sometimes combined with other items, such as a glass rod or a spinning top, and these objects are themselves often sculpted, to show a figure or a creeping insect.

'Glass is a most robust material and withstands the weather in summer and winter. My urge was to take the glass out of the showcases and to put it into the garden, into the landscape. There are engraved garden-glasses on iron pedestals which have lived outdoors for years. You just have to take care of the wind, so they should be in a quiet corner or mounted like a weather-vane.'

LAUF LAUF, FANG FANG ('Run run, catch catch') 12.5cm (5in.) ht x 8cm (3in.) dia
Bowl, lead crystal with ruby red overlay. Sandblasted, engraved and manually polished inside and outside
Photo: Gernot Merker

JAZZ 30cm (11¾in.) ht x 14/19cm (5½/7½in.) width
Clear glass jar with red and blue handle, edge with cuts, sandblasted, engraved, partially polished

Photo: Gernot Merker

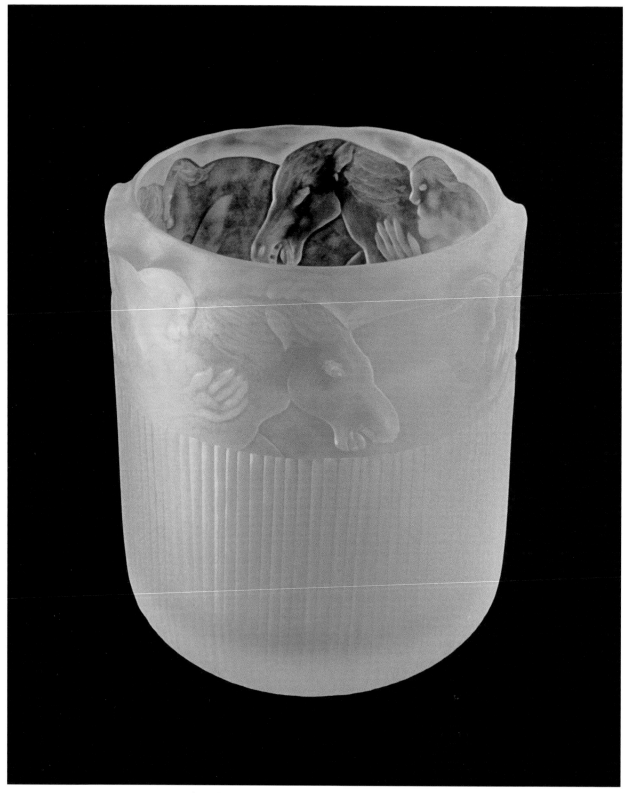

REITERLEIN ('Little horseman') 20cm (8in.) ht x 17cm (6¾in.) dia
Pot, clear lead crystal, sandblasted, engraved and manually polished
Photo: Gernot Merker

DEBORAH O. MEYER (U.S.A.)

THE DANCER 10cm (4in.) x 5cm (2in.) Intaglio engraved lead crystal with cast sterling silver setting

'This pendant is the first in a series of miniature works of art to wear entitled "Windows of the Heart". The dancer represents the beloved who is surrounded by flames symbolising the heart's passion. When worn the dancer represents the wearer's unconscious self; the flames further symbolise the wearer's widening consciousness. The materials themselves, silver and crystal, are a metaphor for the apparent duality of lover and beloved, conscious self and unconscious self.'

From 1973-5, Deb Meyer studied copper-wheel glass engraving with Peter Schelling, engraver with Steuben. From the beginning she studied in drawing, art history, philosophy and religion, and world mythology. In 1975 she studied engraving and other cold-working techniques at Hadamar Glass Art School, West Germany. Between 1976 and 1984 she produced work in her own copper-wheel engraving and cold-working glass studio. From 1994, based in Tucson, Arizona, she

JOURNEY THROUGH
THE DANCE OF
DUALITY

'This is a detail of an installation by Deb and Jon Meyer. The aspects of duality that we all encounter everyday presupposes you and I; light and dark; kiss and kick. This work focuses on the dichotomy of joy and suffering.

'The intaglio engraved figure was carved into a crystal blank which was first hot worked, then cooled, sawn, ground, and polished. The special, rare glass colour was achieved by adding pure gold to the raw glass batch materials, melted in a proprietary process, reheated precisely, and worked to achieve the exact hue desired. Surrounding the glass objects is sand (the basic, primary ingredient in glass), which is a metaphor for unconsciousness, slowly transformed during the journey to the unity beyond duality.'

worked in her own engraving and cold-working glass studio utilising new engraving processes and techniques.

Deborah Meyer's work has been exhibited widely in the U.S.A. and Europe, and features in numerous collections. Examples of her work have been acquired by the Oscar de la Renta Perfume Company in Paris and presented to President Sadat of Egypt., and can be seen in the Burgstrom Mahler Museum, Neena, WI; the Huntington Museum of Art, Huntington WV; the Victoria and Albert Museum, London; Wheaton Museum, Millville, NJ and Woodson Art Museum, Wausau, WI.

STEVEN NEWELL (U.K.)

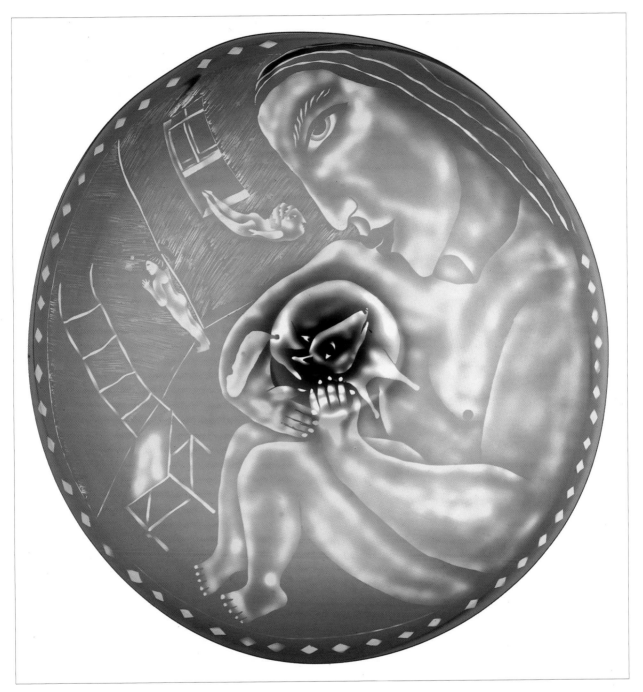

LITTLE FOX 58cm (22¾in.)
Photo: Ed Ironside

'These pieces are all made with the same technique. First Steven Newell blows a large glass charger using inner-case colour. For one-off pieces generally more than one colour is used. Depending on the image he will either create a sharp contrast between the colours or obtain a subtler graduation from one to another.

THE KING'S COUNSEL 65cm (25½in.)
Photo: Ed Ironside

'He then masks the entire charger, cutting out and sandblasting through the inner-case colour systematically to various depths until the image is complete.

'He became interested in working with glass at Carnegie-Mellon University, U.S.A. "I was excited by it because it's transparent, there is an element of it existing and yet not existing." The images are drawn from Biblical tales, Greek myths and well known fables combined with his own personal experience and observation. "If I'm angry or anxious or happy I'll find some historical excuse to use that theme. What is so wonderful about Greek myths is that their themes keep coming back."'

Steven Newell was born in 1948. He attended both Kansas City Art Institute (1969) and Carnegie-Mellon University, completing his B.F.A. degree in Ceramics and Glass in 1972. The same year he was offered and accepted a place at the Royal College of Art, London and completed his M.A. in Glass in 1974. On leaving the Royal College he joined The Glasshouse in Covent Garden, later to become a Director in 1976.

COME DANCING 22.6cm (8¾in.) x 16.2cm (6½in.)
Photo: Karen Norquay

In 1977 he was awarded his first major international prize: the Coburg Glaspreis. At this point he began to evolve two separate directions in his work – repeatable items and highly personal one-off pieces. These now constitute the two main strands to his work. 'Repeatables' are now part of the Newell Glass range and one-offs are shown in major exhibitions and both publicly and privately commissioned works, particularly stained glass windows, cast glass pieces and large installations.

Steven Newell's work has been shown in numerous exhibitions all over the world.

Work in Public Collections
Broadfield House Glass Museum, England; Corning Museum, New York, U.S.A.; the Crafts Council Collection, London; Kunstsammlungen der Veste Coburg, Germany; Museum of Modern Art, Kyoto, Japan; Norwich Castle Museum, Norwich, England; Portsmouth Museum, Portsmouth, England; the Royal Scottish Museum, Edinburgh; Shipley Museum, Tyne and Wear, England; Ulster Museum. Belfast, Northern Ireland; the Victoria and Albert Museum, London;

ISABEL DE OBALDÍA (U.S.A.)

Isabel De Obaldía was born in 1957. She received her B.F.A. from the Rhode Island School of Design in 1979. She is a painter and has been exhibiting individually since 1977. She became interested in glass in the late '80s and attended Pilchuck Glass School in 1987 for the first time. She has returned to Pilchuck several times since and has studied engraving with Jirí Harcuba and Jan Mares. Initially, she engraved and painted on blown vessels, decorating them with the figures and lush vegetation inspired by her paintings. Most recently De Obaldía's interest has moved towards sculpture. She now kiln casts her glass figures and then engraves the pieces with diamond and stone wheels.

She has participated in several glass symposia in Europe and has been invited to exhibit in important international glass exhibitions such as World Glass Now '94. and Venezia Aperto Vetro in 1996.

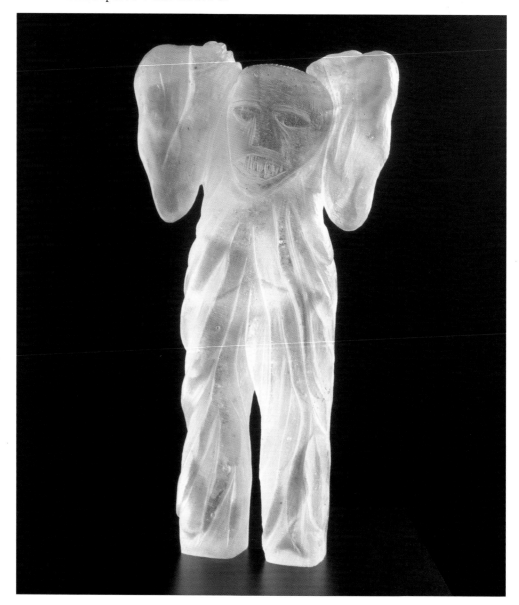

TIGER
38.1cm (15in.) x 20.3cm (8in.) x 7.6cm (3in.)

Kiln cast glass engraved on a lathe with diamond wheels
Photo courtesy of Mary-Anne Martin/Fine Art New York

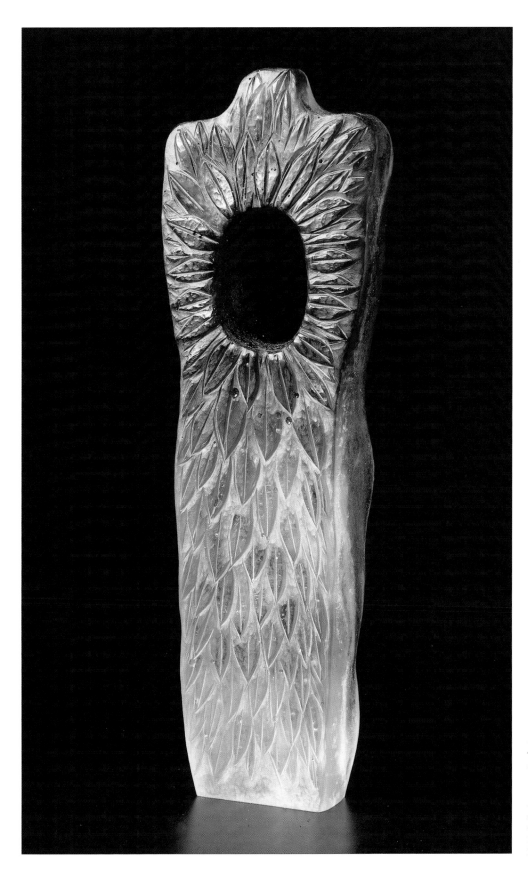

JUAN CALIENTE
36.8cm (14½in.) x 11.6cm
(4½in.) x 9.8cm (4in.)

*Kiln cast glass engraved
on a lathe with diamond
wheels*
Photo courtesy of Mary-Anne
Martin/Fine Art New York

SHIRLEY PALMER F.G.E. (U.K.)

THE ONES THAT GOT AWAY 28cm (11in.) dia
Kiln formed disc and base, drill engraved on both sides of the glass. Drill engraved

'I spent five years at Manchester School of Art exploring the possibilities and problems of painting and of modelling and sculpture before qualifying in both subjects. A period of teaching followed by rearing a family largely put paid to any artistic output. As family commitments decreased I gained a local notoriety as an artist and designer. This included free-

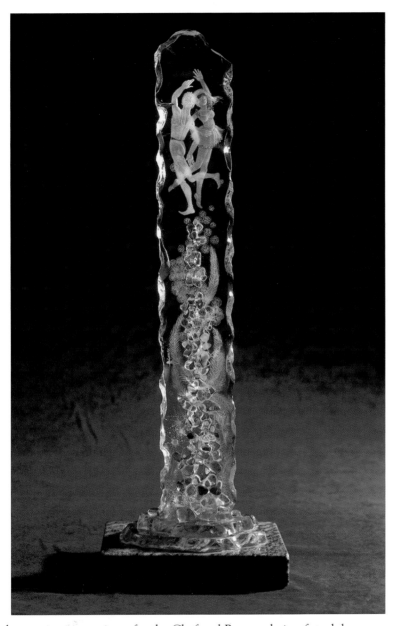

43.2 APOGEE
Float glass pillar with kiln formed additions on marble and glass base. Drill engraved

lance work as an inn sign painter for the Chef and Brewer chain of steak houses.

'Life after a divorce and a return to teaching included an introduction to glass engraving. I married Stuart Palmer and this event coincided with the formation of the Guild of Glass Engravers. We both breathed in some glass dust at the inaugural exhibition and have been addicted ever since. Involvement in the Guild has included a period as Chairman, many exhibitions and the publication of a book on engraving techniques.

'I am interested in technique as well as artistic expression. I have always tried to extend the bounds of engraving and I am fascinated by the challenge of playing with light and colour as part of a design. This has led to the development of a method of laminating coloured glass shapes to a window, door or panel to enrich and complement the engraved imagery. The purchase of a kiln meant that I could take the process one step further and now I make coloured glass pieces specifically designed for engraving.

'The addiction continues!'

141

DAVID PEACE M.B.E., F.S.A., F.G.E. (U.K.)

OBELISK WITH SIX LATIN MOTTOES
Obelisk on glass and gilded base – drill engraved

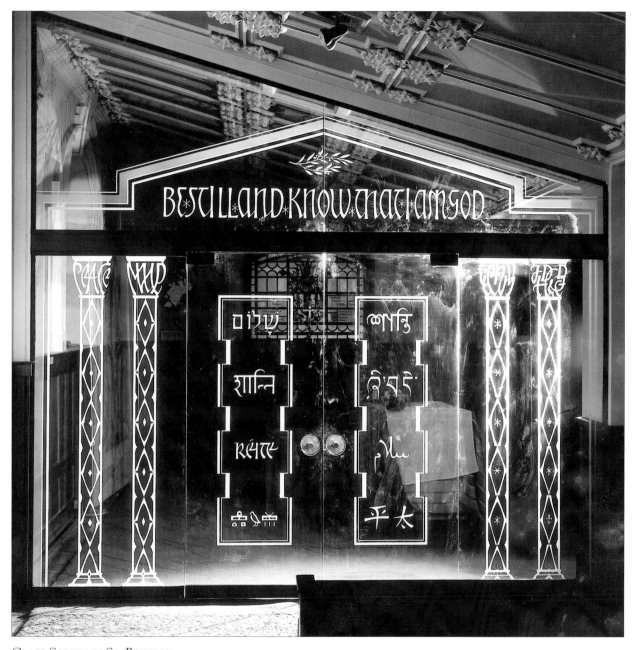

GLASS SCREEN IN ST. BOTOLPH
The screen is in St. Botolph, Aldgate, London, with 'Peace' in eleven languages – sandblasted

David Peace has been engraving since 1935, developing the themes of lettering and heraldry, both in presentation glass at large scale in architecture, notably in windows, screens and doors in churches and cathedrals, including Westminster Abbey. Trained as an architect and by profession a town planner, he has been dedicated to design in all its forms. A former President of the Guild of Glass Engravers and a Past Master of the Artworkers Guild, he has work in many public collections, including the Victoria and Albert Museum, Kettle's Yard Cambridge and the Corning Museum.

RONALD PENNELL (U.K.)

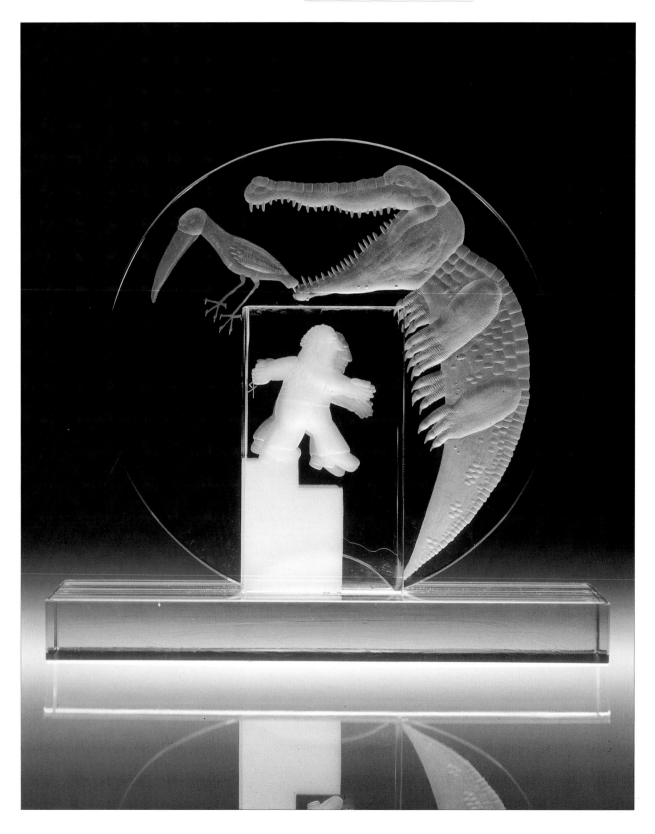

PULLING TOGETHER 25cm (10in.) x 15cm (6in.)
Wheel engraved over graal technique. Green and brown over cased glass.
Photo: Cliff Guttridge F.R.S.A.

'Three men are pulling together to free a friendly serpent from the clutches of Harpies while a Virgin
looks hopefully at the apple. An allegory of human hopes, desires and difficulties with reference to the
way the past comes into the present.'

(Opposite) ON THE EDGE – A REALIZATION OF HUMANIST INTENTION 13.4cm (5¼in.) x 23cm (9in.)
x 21.1cm (8¼in.)
Sculpture, wheel engraved with multiple overlaid images. Glass made in Czech Republic by Moser to the artist's design
Photo: Kazuyuki Okamoto. The piece was acquired by the Hokkaido Museum of Modern Art to commemorate World Glass '94, and
is reproduced here with their kind permission

'The illusion of movement when the man steps forward represents a philosophy important to me:
mankind and the natural world are "on the edge".'

Strange Voyage 17.5cm (6¾in.) x 13cm (5in)
Wheel engraved over graal technique, sage over cased glass.
Photo: Cliff Guttridge F.R.S.A.

'*A voyage into the unknown for this couple and their dog. A bird brings them a fish while two fishermen wield inadequate nets when confronted by a man-headed fish of gigantic proportions. There are stranger creatures lurking in the deep sea…*'

A complete biography lists more than 750 exhibitions world-wide and an extensive bibliography.

1952-56   Birmingham College of Art. (Silversmithing Design and Allied Crafts)
1959   Lecturer, Birmingham College of Art, elected A.R.B.S.A., F.R.S.A.
1964   Left teaching to establish free-lance studio in Herefordshire
1977   Began to engrave glass
1979   Selected for Corning Museum 'WORLD GLASS 'exhibition
          and World Tour 1979-80-81-85-93-95-97. Selected for The Corning
          Museum New Glass Review. One hundred works are selected from a
          world-wide entry
1982   Guest Lecturer: International Glass Symposium, Frauenau, Germany International Glass Symposium, Baden/Vienna; 1st International Glass
          Symposium, Novy Bor, Czechoslovakia
1983   Awarded 2nd Prize, Fragile Art International Glass Competition, San
          Diego, U.S.A.
1988   Engraving Course Leader with Jirí Harcuba, at Pilchuck Glass School,
          U.S.A.
1989   Awarded the Glass Sellers Prize London, with Amanda Brisbane
1990   Founder member of BAFPA and Administrator of the Prize Fund
1992   Invited Artist, International Glass Engraving Symposium, Karlovy Vary,
          Czech Rep.
1993   Awarded a Professorial Fellowship and Gold Medal, Academy of Arts,
          Architecture, and Design Prague.
1990-92-95. Selected for the Kanazawa International Glass Prize exhibitions, Japan
1993   One of ten Invited Foreign Artists, GLASS '93 in Japan, J.G.A.A.
1994   Invited Artist, World Glass Now '94. Hokkaido Museum of Modern Art
1995   Awarded Honorary Membership, Contemporary Applied Arts London
1995   Awarded Finn Lynggaard Prize, 1st Kanazawa International Glass Triennale
1996   Solo exhibition, Lobmeyr Gallery, Vienna
1996   Venezia Aperto Vetro, 1st International Glass Exhibition at the Venice
          Biennale.
1996   Guest Lecturer, 1st International Glass Engraving Symposium, Kamenicky
          Senov. Awarded 'Highest Honour' by the Academy of Arts, Architecture
          and Design Prague, for the most outstanding collaborative work at the
          Symposium
1997   Invited Artist, Hadelands Gallery 'World Glass Exhibition' Norway
1997   Guest Lecturer, 'Bildwerk' Frauenau, Germany

Work in Public Collections
Birmingham University, James Watt Society; British Jewellers Association, London; British Museum, London; Corning Museum of Glass, New York State, U.S.A.; Crafts Council, London; Ebeltoft Museum, Denmark; French National Collection of Contemporary Art, Paris; Glass Museum, Dudley; Goldsmiths Hall, London; Hokkaido Museum of Modern Art, Japan; IGS Collection, Castle Lemberk, Czech Republic; Koganezaki Glass Museum, Japan; H.M.S. *Manchester,* given by Lady Comford; Moser Collection Karlovy Vary, Czech Republic; Museum of Applied Arts, Prague, Czech Republic; Museum of Glass, Kamenicky Senov, Czech Republic; Norwich Castle Museum; Notojima Glass Museum, Japan; Nottingham Castle Museum; Pilchuck Collection at Pacific 1 St Center, Seattle. U.S.A.; Portsmouth City Museum; Turner Museum, Sheffield University; Ulster Museum, Belfast, N. Ireland; Victoria and Albert Museum, London.

STEPHEN PROCTER (U.K.)

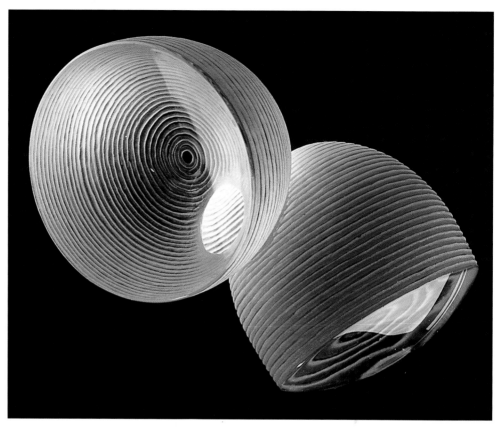

FROM ONE TO THE OTHER 38cm (15in.) x 17cm (6¾in.) x 9cm (3½in.)
Piece in two parts – Small double gathered glass form with optical cutting and engraved surface

'In earlier pieces I used engraving to make the image, to create a world within the form. Recent pieces employ engraving to work the surface of the form so that the piece becomes the experience itself. The process is simple, employing an air driven engraver with different burrs, and then subsequently working the surface by hand, often rubbing it with fine wet and dry paper to introduce the gentle patination of time.'

Stephen Procter's work – by Nola Anderson
'Stephen Procter's art is one of quiet meditation. For him, the work expresses a search for inner harmony, understanding, awareness. The landscape is an important part of Procter's world, and from it he gains insights into his personal search.
   '"When walking through the landscape, it is important to take time to know it well. Working on my vessel forms is a similar journey of discovery. consciously seeking the resonance within." Forms such as *Listening to the River* are Procter's way of searching for possibilities of harmony and balance, expressed through the clarity of the form and enriched and articulated by the vocabulary of light which this medium offers. "It's the stillness, and the empowerment, that is important," says Procter. "It is not passive, rather it is like meditation, a focusing which releases the power within".'

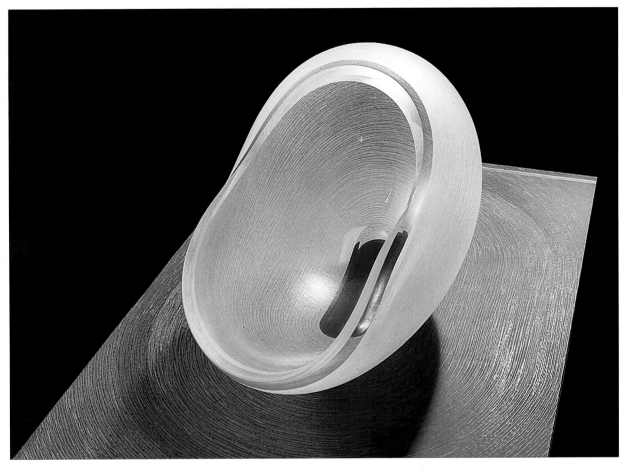

SINGULAR JOURNEY 80cm (31½in.) x 40cm (15¾in.) x 24cm (9½in.)
Piece in three parts – Blown glass rocking form with ground prismatic edge and engraved surface, resting on engraved double glass base

Originally from Britain, Stephen Procter now lives in Australia, where he is head of the Glass Program at Canberra School of Art, part of the Australian National University. He started working with glass as an engraver, moving from images of light to symbolic vessel forms which respond to thoughts about balance and light.

He has lived for a period in the U.S.A., teaching at Illinois State University; has exhibited his work internationally and is represented in many significant collections.

1970	Established own engraving studio, Ashburton, Devon
1976	Major Bursary Award from Crafts Council
1977	Visiting Artist, Glass Studio Franzensbad, Baden, Austria
1978-9	Artist in Residence at Illinois State University, U.S.A. for 1½ years.
1979-81	Artist in Residence (Glass) with Northern Arts/Sunderland Polytechnic.
1980-84	Visiting Lecturer at the Royal College of Art
1981-91	Moved to Farnham, Surrey. Senior Lecturer at West Surrey College of Art and Design. Established own studio near Farnham
1991-92	Visiting Associate Professor (Acting Head of Glass) Illinois State University, U.S.A.
1992	Appointed Head of Glass Workshop, the Australian National University Institute of the Arts, Canberra School of Art, Australia
1994-95	Established new studio near Canberra

LISTENING TO THE RIVER II 60cm (23½in.) dia x 36cm (14in.)
Piece in three parts – blown glass form with ground prismatic edge and engraved surface, resting on engraved double glass base

1995	Started Glass Canberra Technical Data base on the internet
1996-97	Initiated Australian Glass on the World Wide Web http://www.anu.edu.au/ITA/CSA/Glass/Glass.Canberra
1997	Australia Council 'New Work' project grant

Work in Public Collections
Augustiner Museum, Freiburg, Germany; The Borowsky Collection of Contemporary Glass, Philadelphia, U.S.A.; The Brunnier Gallery and Museum, Iowa, U.S.A.; City Art Gallery, Wagga Wagga, Australia; Corning Museum of Glass, Corning, New York, U.S.A.; Crafts Council, London, U.K.; Ebeltoft Glasmuseum, Denmark; Hergiswiler Glas Collection, Lucerne, Switzerland; Illinois State University, Illinois, U.S.A.; Immenhausen Glas Museum, Immenhausen, Germany; Kunstammlungen Der Veste Coburg, Germany; Kunstmuseum Düsseldorf, Germany; Lobmeyr Collection, Vienna, Austria; Museum Bellerive, Zurich, Switzerland; Museum of Decorative Art, Lausanne, Switzerland; National Gallery of Victoria, Australia; National Museum of Modern Art, Kyoto, Japan; News International Corporation, Australia; Novy Bor Symposium Collection, Lemberk Castle, Czech Republic; Royal Albert Memorial Museum, Exeter, U.K.; Royal Museum of Scotland, Edinburgh, U.K.; Schweizerische Kreditanstalt Bank, Luzern, Switzerland; Shipley Art Gallery and Museum, Gateshead, U.K.; Victoria and Albert Museum, London, U.K.

DAVID PRYTHERCH (U.K.)

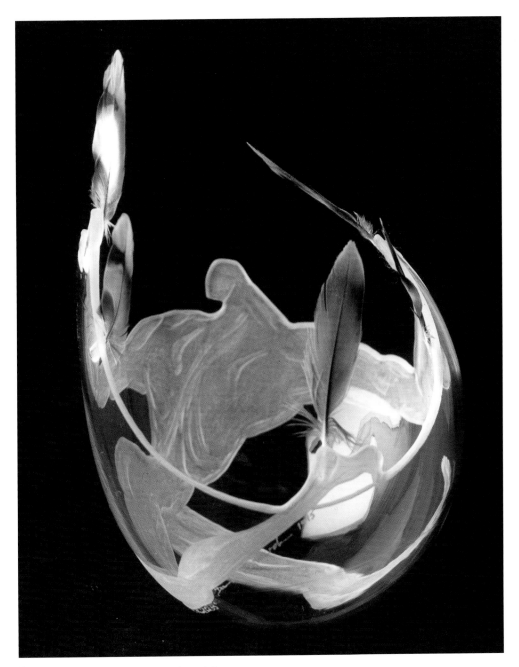

JUGGLER WITH FEATHERS 16cm (6¼in.) dia
Drill engraved on very thin sculptured glass

This is a 16mm (½in.) bubble which has been blown to make the glass very thin and delicate. It also makes it extremely difficult to engrave, as it shatters very easily when cut with a diamond burr. One of the artist's well-known rocking pieces, it dances in the slightest puff of wind. 'What activity could be harder to do than juggling with feathers? – An allegory of life as a free-lance artist – or a free-lance anything!' The feathers are real, and are set into the glass.

MARK RAYNES ROBERTS (Canada)

ETERNAL VISION 30.5cm (12in.) x 45.7cm (18in.) x 17.8cm (7in.)

'The sterling silver figurine depicts doves encircling a wave out of which branches appear. Set within the top branches of the figurine is a 478 carat Brazilian aquamarine, the gemstone which represents the sea and youth. The natural splendour of the stone is framed within the unnatural beauty of the optical lead crystal. Hand carved on to each triangle is a three-dimensional image, symbolising life, hope, light and the children of the world.

'The concept, design and execution of "Eternal Vision" took several months, my greatest challenge being to combine the four individual materials into a work of art that would be in harmony. The aquamarine is the guiding force, the crystal and silver reaching up towards that power, as the children reach up their hands in search of guidance. More than ever, there is a great concern towards the environment and man's destruction of the world. In this piece I wanted to convey respect towards the earth and a need for direction towards the unknown course that lies ahead.'

Mark Raynes Roberts was born in England and trained as a silversmith and hand engraver at the Birmingham School of Jewellery and Silversmithing, where he worked under Ronald Pennell. He received the British Jewellers Association's top

ETERNITY 28cm (11in.) x 23cm (9in.) x 3.8cm (1½in.)
Diamond wheel and stipple engraved

'The end is the beginning. Cocooned in gossamer, spirits soar and the soul lives on forever.'

award four times for engraving and design. Having emigrated to Canada in 1982, he became a Canadian citizen in 1988. His work can be found in numerous royal, corporate and private collections throughout the world, and the Raynes Crystal Collection is on permanent display in Orangeville, Toronto.

JACQUES RUIJTERMAN F.G.E. (The Netherlands)

THE UPPER GALLERY
Diamond point and diamond and carborundum wheel engraved on large goblet

'People at a modern art exhibition'

Started engraving in 1979
Six years' apprenticeship and co-operation with Tim Appleyard

WAITING
Diamond point and diamond wheel engraved on large goblet

Elected Fellow of the Guild of Glass Engravers 1985
Started commercial studio glass and engraving studio in Arundel, West Sussex

155

MARE SAARE (Estonia)

DEALING WITH CHAOS 32cm (12½in.) x 32cm (12½in.) x 4cm (1½in.)
Acid-etched, slumped engraved on black glass

'Both acid and heat are very unpredictable working companions. My first impulses to control them have passed, my trust in them has increased. I let the chemical reactions, caused by acid and heat, create the chaos, just as, to some extent, I have to give up control over what's happening in my life, only to take it in my own hands again and deal with the chaos to the best of my knowledge.'

THE UNEXPLAINED 33.5cm (13¼in.) x 33.5cm (13¼in.)
Acid-etched and slumped on black glass

'Black glass is so different from the glass we are used to. It doesn't have the main property of "normal" glass – transparency. But it acts like glass – responds to hydrofluoric acid, bends and reacts in heat.

'I do not want to tell a story. For some time now I have been asking questions, and now step by step, I'm receiving answers. The richness of black glass, its subtlety and tenderness give me limitless material for the dialogue.'

THE JOURNEY 25cm (10in.) dia
Cased glass, blown, acid-etched and engraved

'Many of my later works bear the name "Journey". This is the first one of the series and during my journey there have been, and will be, more.'

'I work in fusing techniques, as well as acid-etching, engraving, cutting, stained and painted glass, hot techniques. The images are of the very hectic, unstable, most important changes in the life of my homeland and its people. The turning point in my connections with the world, with information coming in, uncertainty, disturbance, knowledge…the world coming closer and becoming accessible…

'I enjoy the graphic properties of the acid-etching process and the absolute control of the engraving.'

1974-1979	Estonian State Art Institute (now the Estonian Academy of Arts)
1980	Designer, Kaluga glass factory, Russia
Since 1984	Member of the Estonian Artists' Association
1985-1993	Assistant, the Estonian Academy of Arts, dept of glass
1993	Hot glass course, Bornholm glass school, Denmark
Since 1993	Associate Professor, head of the dept of glass, the Estonian Academy of Arts
1995	Post-graduate studies, the Royal College of Art, London

Works in public collections
Estonian Applied Arts Museum, Estonian History Museum, Tallinn City Museum, Estonian Sports Museum, Estonian Art Foundation, the History Museum of Tartu University, the Lääne-Nigula Church, the Estonian Ministry of Justice, Tallinn, Estonia; Gus-Khrustalny Crystal Museum, Vladimir region, Russia; Kamenicky Senov Glass museum, Czechia; Lviv Glass Museum, Ukraine; V. Polenov Museum, Polenovo, Russia; private collections.

BARRY SAUTNER (U.S.A.)

DECIDUOUS DESIRES
19.4cm (7½in.) ht
9.5cm (3¾in.) dia

'This sculpture was carved from a vase consisting of a layer of white over crystal over blue glass. The entire surface of the white vase was covered with a resist tape. My design was drawn and then traced over with a razor knife. The resist tape was removed from the negative spaces surrounding my design, and the white glass sandblasted down until the blue layer was revealed.

'The resist tape covering the design was removed from the white surface revealing a white silhouette of my design. This remaining white was sandblasted freehand into a bas-relief form with some undercutting at the edges and under some of the vines.

'The blue background was then sandblasted freehand piercing the blue layer. This resulted in blue branches behind the white branches making it appear as the forest behind the figures.

'The human form trapped within trees represents the spirituality and higher consciousness of nature. On the reverse side the male "tree spirit" reaches out tapping the female "tree spirit" on the shoulder with his branches, and she has turned around looking over her shoulder. On the front side the two "tree spirits" are embracing each other and the ivy vine has tied them together. This unity has resulted in the female "tree spirit" sprouting her first leaves of spring.'

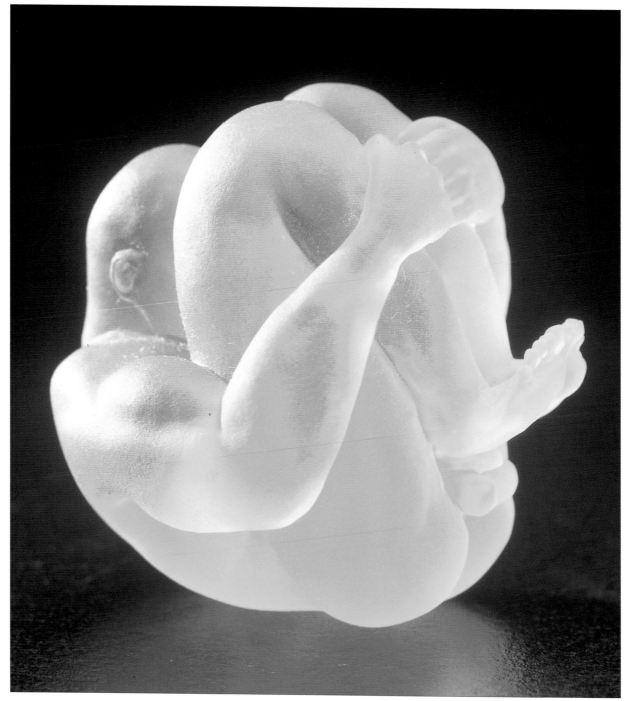

UMBILICAL MALE 5cm (2in.) dia

'This carving of a male nude in a foetal position was carved from a glass sphere freehand using sandblasting. The sandblasting equipment is a technically refined machine. I use a fine grade of aluminium oxide powder, and the "pencil blaster" has nozzles with orifices as small as three one-thousandths of an inch.'

'This design came to me at a time when my life was in need of change. This form represents the need to look within oneself in order to change and be reborn.'

FORBIDDEN FRUIT
10.6 cm (4in.) x 10.5 cm
(4in.) x 3.2 cm (1¼in.)

'This sculpture was carved from a glass sphere consisting of a layer of white over a layer of blue over a crystal core. The top and bottom of this sphere were ground into a wafer shape on a grinding wheel until all three colours could be seen on both sides, and then these flat surfaces were polished. One side of the white was ground flat, enabling the wafer to stand on end.

'The resulting wafer was covered with a special resist tape made specifically for sandblasting. I then drew my design on to the tape and traced over this design with a razor knife. The tape was removed from the total front surface of the crystal core, and from my design on the rear surface of the crystal core. I then sandblasted my design into the crystal from behind into a three dimensional carving within the crystal consisting of a serpent wound around an apple tree. The two crystal surfaces were then covered again with the resist tape protecting them until the piece was finished.

'The resist tape was then removed from the area surrounding the design drawn on the white surface. All of the white glass surrounding this design was sandblasted down to the blue layer. The remaining resist tape covering the design was then removed revealing a white silhouette of the design which was then sandblasted freehand into a three dimensional male and female, and two doves.

'The layer of blue was then sandblasted freehand into branches and leaves, and then hollowed out until the blue glass no longer touched the crystal core with the exception of a small post at the bottom of the crystal.

'Finer and finer grades of powder were used until the surface had a satin finish.

'This sculpture is my interpretation of the story of Adam and Eve. It represents Man's struggle with temptation and with himself. I believe that Man and Woman together will ultimately overcome temptation and then become reunited with "THE ONE".'

GERNOT SCHLUIFER (Austria)

LEOPARD ON TREE 30cm (11¾in.) x 30 cm (11¾in.)
Copper wheel engraving, coloured and plated with gold, combined with Porphyroide from the Alps, about 650 million years old

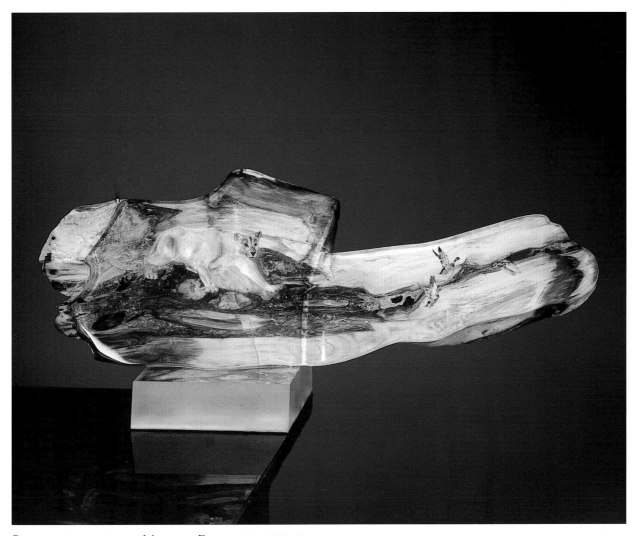

PUMA TRYING TO CATCH MALLARD DUCKS 60cm (23½in.)
Copper wheel engraving, plated with gold and combined with petrified Ginkgo wood, about 180 million years old

'After many years of creating works of art from glass, I have now embarked on totally new and innovative methods for combining glass with stone in the conception of sculptures and engravings.

'As an observant admirer of nature, I am fascinated by the works of art which nature presents to us: stones, avalanches, rivers, creeks, and canyons. In particular, rocks arising from iced-up waters inspired me to combine glass and stone.

'The result is a selection of fine art images of wildlife and nature, relating to my years of living in a magnificent environment, my respect for nature, and my love of art. My unique combination with stones, some as much as 600 million years old, has been developed to create lasting works of art.

'My basic concept is that art must be beautiful – enjoyable to the eye, to the hand, and to the soul. My sculptures have to be touched for the full realization of their tactile appeal, evoking sensuous and almost erotic feelings.

'In addition, I am creating a wide selection of miniatures and jewellery in combinations of gemstones with glass engravings. The attractiveness of these designs is everlasting.'

MAPLE LEAF WITH LIZARDS 25cm (10in.) x 20cm (8in.) x 10cm (4in.)
Copper wheel engraving, coloured and plated with gold and different metals, two layers of optical glass combined with Magmatite

1955 – 1958   Glasacademie in Kramsach/Austria
1958 – 1965   Worked together with a Bohemian master in Kramsach
Since 1965   Working as a free-lance artist

Work in Public Collections
Art Museum, Valencia; Corning Museum of Glass, Corning, U.S.A.; Ministerium für Kunst und Kultur, Wien; Musée des Arts Décoratifs, Lausanne; Museo Municipal de Arte en vidrio Contemporáneo Ciudad de Alcarcón, Madrid; Museum of Fine Arts, Robert O. Kinsey Collection, Anchorage, Alaska; Tiroler Landesmuseum, Innsbruck, Austria.

CHRISTIAN SCHMIDT (Germany)

ISN'T MY SWEET LITTLE THING PRETTY? 25cm (9¾in.) dia
Overlay, wheel engraving
Photo: Lisa Moser

'Scenes-Space in Glass' by Katharina Eisch, Frauenau
'Glass engraving cannot be considered simply an antiquated craft. In Christian Schmidt's hands it becomes a narrative medium for a magician in glass. Every cut of the engraving wheel is spontaneous and irreversible. One needs thoughtful certainty and precision. The design and graphic qualities of the glass engraving encourage representational associations, and their sensibility leads one to a study of details.

'At first, the viewer is absorbed with the complexity of the foreground and background; light and shadow; and the contrasting effect of the engraved and sandblasted surface. With closer examination, complex scenes and figures come to life. Fluid forms which appear non-representative and accidental flow into faces, limbs, bodies or a ship full of human and animal creatures – each dense and communicating its own story.

'Christian Schmidt is interested in everything human, including the grotesque. We are not confronted with a fantastic dream world, a compact narrative out of mythological folk tales or a science fiction milieu, rather a very private perspective from an individual who scrutinises us with myriad eyes. We are treated to aspects of contemporary life – an every-day, banal, petty

MANUAL
LIGHTNING
RECEIVER
20cm (7¾in.) ht
Overlay, engraving

bourgeois contemporary life with perhaps a certain sense of irony; or the scope of a self-referential epoch – known yet suddenly alien. Glass is not simply a neutral canvas for drawing. The hollow glass form, as well as the effect of lithophane, create a three-dimensional space. With each turn of the vessel, the observer views an ever-changing surface created by the layering, as well as the perspective viewed through the vessel. The development of the narrative remains in question, and the protagonists fade into the fluid, glassy background out of which they emerged.'

1974-77	Staatl. Glasfachschule Zwiesel (Technical Glass College – craft of engraving)
1977-85	Engraver with various glass works
1986	Installed his own studio in Rabenstein/Zwiesel

Awards

1988	2. Bayerwald-Glaspreis, 2nd. Prize, Free Glass-Art, Glass Museum, Frauenau
1993	Bayerwald-Glaspreis 1993, Honorary Prize, Glass Museum, Frauenau
1995	The International Exhibition of Glass Kanazawa, Gold-Prize, Kanazawa, Japan
1996	Kulturförderpreis Ostbayern
	Daniel-Swarovski-Prize, Honorary Prize, 1st International Symposium Engraved Glass, Kamenicky Senov, Czech Republic

CONJUNCTIONS 22cm (8¾in.) ht
Overlay, engraving
Photo Lisa Moser

'The technique used (for all three examples) is wheel-engraving using diamond, carborundum or silicon-carbide wheels.

'The technique "Lithophane" is believed to have been innovated in Meissen in 1827. The term is usually used to refer to an unglazed thin porcelain plate with an intaglio design. The transparency of the porcelain in combination with the design in relief create light and dark areas when held up to the light. Although this technique was used for a short period of time it faded again into obscurity. In the early 1990s Christian Schmidt discovered the lithophane technique again using it to create his masterpieces.'

Work in Public Collections
Collection Herrmann, Drachselsried; the Corning Museum of Glass, Corning, N.Y.; Ernsting Foundation, Alter Hof Herding, Coesfeld; Glass Museum, Frauenau; Glass Museum Immenhausen; Glass Museum, Kamenicky Senov, Czech Republic; Glass Museum, Wertheim; Hokkaido Museum of Modern Art, Japan; Kunstsammlung Ostbayern, Spital Hengersberg; Museum of Art, Marquette University, Milwaukee; Museum of Art, New Orleans, LA; Württembergisches Landesmuseum, Stuttgart; Waldmuseum Zwiesel.

SALLY SCOTT F.G.E. (U.K.)

IMAGES OF RAJASTHAN 79cm (31in.) dia
Clear crystal spun glass disc. Sandblasted and drill engraved and painted. The crescent moon support is steel set in a slate base.
Photo: Nick Carter

'*The design was inspired by a recent trip to Rajasthan.*'

Sally Scott trained as a painter at Croydon College of Art and The Royal Academy Schools. Since the 1980s, her exploration of different media has led her into a special interest in the use of glass and the development of a variety of techniques for illustrative work in this medium.

MOON LILY 54cm (21¼in.) dia
Blue flashed spun glass disc. Sandblasted and drill engraved

Photo: Nick Carter

*'The white Moon Lily flowers only at night, the glorious deep blue of this glass was the inspiration for
this piece.'*

'In memory of Emma Sclater depicting Creation and reflecting her love of architecture. The sun and moon at the top with a cosmic spiral containing the five "Platonic solids" as the basis of all form, leading down to a fallen Corinthian column with a real Acanthus (in colour) rising up from the stone Acanthus decoration in the capital.'

Work

Design commissions, primarily for public buildings such as churches and colleges (mostly in conjunction with architects but also for private clients) using techniques of sandblasting, engraving and painting.

Independent commissions have included: West doors for Leicester Cathedral; Doors to the Church of St. James, Whitehaven; Windows for the Church of St.Andrew, Thornton Heath; Fanlight, Church of Our Lady and St.Michael, Abergavenny; West doors, Church of St. Peter and St. Paul, Chingford. Screens have also been commissioned by international hotel groups, Royal Brierley Crystal, the Royal Albert Hall and the Victoria and Albert Museum.

Sally Scott formed a partnership with David Peace (q.v.), which combines their complementary skills for work on a number of joint commissions since 1986. Some of the more recent include: Panel for The Turner Glass Museum, Sheffield; Windows for the Church of St. Andrew, Headington, Oxford; Chapel doors for Lincoln College, Oxford; West doors to Westminster Abbey.

LADA SEMECKÁ (Czech Republic)

GREAT EATING
15cm (6in.) x 20cm
(8in.)
*Copper wheel engraved
on crystal vase after a
painting by Mikolás
Medek*

1987-1991 Artistic School of Glass Kamenicky Senov
1991-1992 Engraver at Moser, Karlovy Vary
1992-1994 Institute of Applied Arts, Ústí Nad Labem
Since 1994 University of Applied Arts, Prague
1996 International symposium of engraved glass Kamenicky Senov

TRACEY SHEPPARD F.G.E. (U.K.)

'I began engraving at evening classes in 1980 whilst studying for a B.A. Hons degree in Fine Art and English Literature. The opportunities offered by this transparent canvas fascinated me. There are endless possibilities for creating three-dimensional illusions and using light to bring images to life.

'In 1982 I graduated, the Guild of Engravers accepted me as a craft member and I began work as an engraver. I was elected a Fellow in 1987.

'Now I work from a studio in my home in Winchester. On glass I can indulge my love of drawing from the natural world, closely observing the structure and fine detail of botanical subjects. This interest has led to many commissions from plant collectors and botanists, in particular the Hillier Trophy for Southern England in Bloom.

'I also enjoy working with textural and tonal variations and the joys of perspective, often on a curved surface. The Dean and Chapter of Salisbury Cathedral have commissioned several views of the Spire and the Close. The Civil Aviation Authority demands were more rigorous – a largely glass and steel building on a glass block. I am often asked to engrave houses and their gardens and thoroughly enjoyed a commission to capture a view of Birkhall for Queen Elizabeth the Queen Mother in 1996.

'The discipline of heraldic subjects is satisfying. A chalice engraved for Ampleforth posed design problems, and the light bulb engraved with the BBC's coat of arms was a technical headache.

'I find large scale projects exciting. The first of these was for Sandle Manor School in Hampshire, who commissioned four memorial windows which feature architecture, plants, wildlife and lettering. The Church of St James the Great in Wiltshire commissioned three memorial panels illustrating the story of five barley loaves and two fish; these had to be woven in with the bell ringing and bee keeping interests of one parishioner – I relish a challenge!

'There are so many avenues to explore. I would like to work more with coloured glass and to continue to explore the humorous combination of words and images. I have recently experimented with combining sandblast and drill techniques whilst designing and engraving the window for the Dovecote at the Wessex Children's Hospice. This is a mixture of techniques I would like to explore further. For me the possibilities of engraving are limited only by my lifespan.'

SUMMER '95   27.5cm (10¾in.) dia
Drill engraved

THE DEANERY 27cm (10½in.) x 20.5cm (8in.) dia
Drill engraved

Photo reproduced with the kind permission of the Very Reverend Michael Till and Mrs. Till

PUFF THE MAGIC DRAGON 13cm (5in.) dia
Drill engraved

MARY STEVENS F.G.E. (U.K.)

NIGHT 25cm (10in.) ht
Copper wheel engraved with diamond-point stars on dark brown oval vase

'*When humanity sleeps and creatures of the night take command*'

CRYSTAL AMETHYST 30cm (11¾in.)
Copper wheel engraved on both sides of cased amethyst disc, slate base

'Design inspired by crystal formations in natural amethyst'

HARVEST MOUSE 7.5cm (3in.) dia
Three-dimensional copper wheel engraving on paperweight.

'The mouse is life size'

Mary Stevens trained at Stourbridge College of Art and Royal College of Art London, specialising in glass for her final qualifications. She has worked with glass for over thirty years, firstly as a designer in the glass industry before embarking on a free-lance career. Her work has been in numerous exhibitions, and pieces are now in private collections around the world.

Mary uses a variety of techniques, her speciality being copper wheel engraving – a difficult technique to master, and now practised by only a small minority of engravers. She enjoys exploring a wide range of subjects for interpretation into both figurative and abstract designs.

TAKEO TAKEMASA (Japan)

CELLO PLAYER 17cm (6¾in.) x 25cm (10in.) ht
Copper wheel engraved
Photo: Frank J. Borkowski

DANCING 42cm (16½in.) x 28.5cm (11¼in.) ht
Copper wheel engraved

The design and engraving skills of Takeo Takemasa have appeared on glass objects created by leading artistic glass companies in America and in Japan. The creativity of his designs and the artistry of his engraving have enriched objects in the major collections of art glass in Europe, America, and Japan. His engraving skills have enhanced presentation pieces which are now in the collections of a number of private collectors as well as of royal palaces, and his abilities are widely recognised in the world of glass.

1975-1977	Part-time glass blower at the Ida Glass Factory in Tokyo, Japan
1977-1978	Studied copper wheel glass engraving as well as other related glass-making skills and glass history on a Carl Duisberg Scholarship in West Germany
1978-1982	Trained in copper-wheel glass engraving design, and drawing at the Kramsach Glass School in Austria
1982-1989	Employed as a Master copper-wheel Glass Engraver at Steuben Glass, Corning, New York
1989-	Free-lance designer and engraver on glass

HILARY VIRGO F.G.E. (U.K.)

'After a career as a painter and designer of stage costumes, mainly for musicals and revue, I began engraving glass in about 1975, enjoying the three-dimensional quality of a medium which allows for both draughtsmanship and sculpture, but with the discipline of a given shape. Early medieval painting and carving is a great source of inspiration and example, particularly in the figure form. The piece shown here, however, evolved from the idea of fat ladies and a technique for engraving steam – the result was a Turkish bath.'

STEAMING
Drill engraved dome and moulded disc

ANNE WENZEL (Germany)

FERRARI 13.5cm (5¼in.) ht x 41cm (16in.) x 3.4 cm (1¼in.)
Flat glass, sawn, cut and polished, sand blasted, deep engraved using stones and diamonds

1974-77   Staatl. Glasfachschule Hadamar, Hessen, Dept. Glass engraving
1977-79   Active in Baden-Württemberg and Schleswig-Holstein
Since 1979 Personal studio in Flensburg
1982   Master's Degree, Mitglied der ADK-Schleswig-Holstein

Work in Public Collections
Glasmuseum, Kamenicky Senov; Glasmuseum, Wertheim; Worms Museum;
Württembergisches Landesmuseum, Stuttgart.

DEVIL SHUTTLE 22.3cm (8¾in.) ht x 24cm (9½in.) x 3.4cm (1¼in.)
Flat glass, sawn, cut and polished, sand blasted, deep engraved using stones and diamonds

'A frequent subject is again and again the theme "human being in a car on the way". The car, well known as "the Germans' most popular child", becomes here the synonym for the yearning for distant destinations, for mobility, modernity and prosperity. Simultaneously it is also an alcove as well as a protection area and private space. In his car, the mobile person feels private, yet he is publicly present. In Ferrari and Devil Shuttle, the car is always more than just a locomotive means. It is also living room, showpiece object and cult figure. It is a mirror of the little everyday dreams.

'With the Greek Theatre a classic topic is being taken up. The silhouette-like dream is in contrast to the dreary reality, the dreamlike princess to the illusionless but real cleaning lady.'

GREEK THEATRE 23.8cm (9½in.) ht x 40cm (15¾in.) x 15.5cm (6in.)
Flat glass, deep engraved using stones and diamonds, sandblasted, black enamel painting

LAURENCE WHISTLER C.B.E., F.G.E. (U.K.)

DORSET NIGHTFALL 6.4cm (2½) dia
Bowl – stipple engraved

Laurence Whistler revived point engraving in 1934, and is the Founder President of the Guild of Glass Engravers. The importance of his influence both on countless engravers and on the revival of the art form over the years can hardly be overstated. It was after inscribing a poem with a diamond tool on a sheet of glass in a friend's house, and the work that followed as a result, that he realised that he was not inventing a new craft, but reviving an ancient one. His subsequent researches into the glass engraving practised in England and Holland in the seventeenth and eighteenth centuries revealed the extent to which a great art form had all but become extinct in England. His work, on a wide range of subjects

AN OVERFLOWING LANDSCAPE 25.4cm (10in.) dia
Bowl – drill engraved

'*On the bedroom wall (engraved inside the bowl), the picture has expanded into a landscape (engraved outside) which flows round and invades the room.*'

– landscapes, moonlight, sunlight, buildings and poetically-inspired themes, is to be seen in museums and private collections all over the world. His books, containing his writings on the engravings, together with flawless photography, have inspired engravers and non-engravers alike. He has executed commissions

TO THE POET EDWARD THOMAS

'In Eastbury Church near Lambourn.'

for The Queen and the Queen Mother, and his work has been acquired by the
Victoria and Albert Museum, the Ashmolean Museum, the Fitzwilliam Museum,
Cambridge, the Royal Scottish Museum, the Museum of Art, Philadelphia, the
Corning Museum and numerous other collections.

SIMON WHISTLER F.G.E. (U.K.)

CLAUDE AT STOWE
9cm (3½in.) dia
Stipple engraved goblet

'Claude Lorrain's painting "Pastoral Caprice" with his original buildings replaced by three from the landscape garden at Stowe.'

Simon Whistler first learnt engraving from his father Laurence, beginning with simple heraldic and inscriptional ideas in line engraving. During four years at Stowe school, he developed a love of architecture, particularly ruins, in a landscape setting, which together with pure landscape remains his principal source of inspiration. By the time he went to the Royal Academy of Music in London as a serious music student he was attempting more elaborate architectural subjects in stipple.

His landscape compositions owe much to his interest in the watercolour artists of the late eighteenth and early nineteenth centuries, as well as displaying his father's influence, who provided many early designs. These compositions can have

TEMPLA QUAM DILECTA 30.5cm (12in.) dia
Stipple engraved bowl

'Forty-three garden buildings from Stowe'

real elements in their overall form, or can be purely imaginary.

Most of Simon Whistler's work has been commissioned by private collectors. One piece, the *Finzi Bowl*, engraved jointly with his father, is in the Ashmolean Museum in Oxford. Another, a landscape, is in the Corning Museum of Glass in America.

189

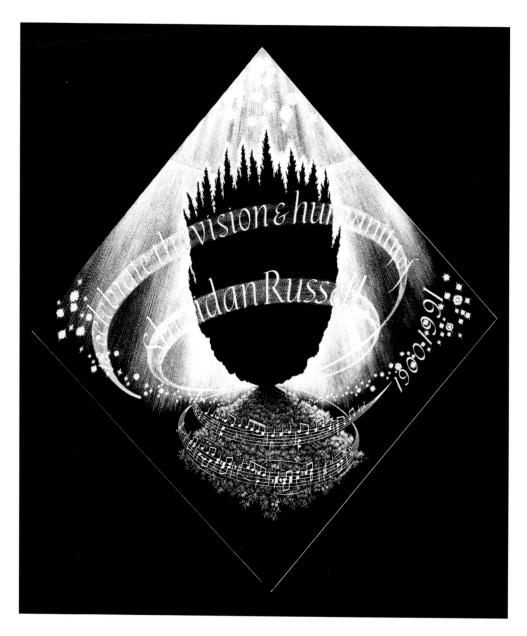

DIAMOND PANE IN
CHRIST CHURCH,
CHELSEA IN
MEMORY OF
SHERIDAN RUSSELL
76.2cm (30in.) ht

Stipple engraved

Most of his work has been done on goblets but other engraved forms have been undertaken – window panes, plates and decanters. Two examples of larger compositions exist in a Memorial Window in St Mary's Church, Funtington, West Sussex, and in Buckland Abbey, South Devon. The latter was commissioned by the National Trust to commemorate the 400th anniversary of the Armada in 1988. With his life combining two disciplines – that of engraving and that of a professional viola player, engravings with a musical subject are a not unexpected result. Two examples are the *Lark Ascending* and the *Finzi Bowl* mentioned above. Two more examples were engraved in 1991 to celebrate the bicentenary of Mozart's death.

Simon Whistler is a Fellow of the Society of Designer-Craftsmen, and a Fellow of the Guild of Glass Engravers, of which he is a founder member and with whom he has exhibited many times.

190

ANN WOLFF (Germany)

THE NUMBER IS TWO 25cm (9¾in.) dia
Cup – sculpture – multicoloured underlay, blown glass etched and sandblasted

Photo: Anders Qwarnström. Reproduced by kind permission of the Victoria and Albert Museum, London

MOTHER OF THE OPEN FIELDS 35cm (13⅛in.) dia
Bowl – multicoloured underlay, blown glass etched and sandblasted

Photo: Anders Qwarnström

1937   b. Lübeck, Germany (1959-1985 Ann Wärff)
1956-59   Studied visual communication at Hochschule für Gestaltung in Ulm,
            Germany
1960-64   Designer at Pukebergs Glasbruk, Nybro, Sweden
1964-78   Designer at Kosta Boda, Sweden
1978-1983   Own Glas Studiohütte in Transjö, Sweden
1982   Co-founder of Transjö-Hytta in Transjö, Sweden
since 1981 Own studio for painting, sculpture and glass
1977 – 1979 – 1984 – 1986 – 1995 Faculty member at Pilchuck Glass Center,
            Stanwood, Seattle
since 1993 Professor for decorative arts and cognitive design at the Art Academie,
            Hamburg, Germany

Awards include: Lunningprize (for Scandinavia); Coburger Glaspreis, Germany (first winner);
Zentralschweitzer Glaspreis (1st and 3rd Prize); Ehrenpreis, International Glasart, Kassel,
Germany; Worlds Crafts Council Glasprize, Bratislava CSSR; Bayrischer Staatspreis
Goldmedaille, München, Germany; Rakow Commission for the Corning Museum of Glass.
   Ann Wolff's work can be seen in collections and exhibitions worldwide.

BIRD – GODDESS 75cm (29½in.) ht
Sculpture – multicoloured underlay, blown glass etched and sandblasted
Photo: Gunnar Böttger

HIROSHI YAMANO (Japan)

FROM EAST TO
WEST, FISH IN THE
WATER – OKE
45cm (17¾in.) x 22cm
(8¾in.) x 14cm 5½in.)
*Blown glass, engraved,
glued, copper plated, cut
and polished*

*'This piece's shape is
influenced by
Japanese old water
container, OKE'*

194

FROM EAST TO
WEST, FISH IN THE
WATER – HITO
57cm (22½in.) x 16cm
(6¼in.) x 12cm (4¾in.)
*Blown glass, engraved,
glued, copper plated, cut
and polished*

'*This piece's shape is
based on the human
figure*'

FROM EAST TO
WEST
75cm (29½in.) x 20cm
(8in.) x 20cm (8in.)
*Blown glass, engraved,
glued, copper plated, cut
and polished*

'I apply thick silver leaf on to the glass surface when the glass is hot and fuse it by using hot glass technique. After annealing in the kiln for a week, I use a hand diamond engraving tool and draw my images. To some parts of the silver surface I apply copper plating and use Japanese old-time patina "kokushiyo" to change the colour to copper.'

'My fish makes excursions all his life, because that is his destiny. I feel the same way. All existence is governed by the rule of the universe. The universe keeps circular motion. My existence is based on the circle. I will keep swimming like my fish, because tomorrow will be fine.'

LIST OF ENGRAVERS

Affolter, Konrad
Kramgasse 9
CH-3011 Bern
Switzerland

Ainslie, Chris
105 Woodmancote
Yate
Bristol
BS17 4LH
U.K.

Berkeley, Betty
La Haute Siguenie
Petit Bersac
24600 Riberac
France

Borowski, Pawel
Glasstudio Borowski
GmbH
Heckelsberg 4
D-53773 Hennef
Germany

Borowski, Stanislaw
Glasstudio Borowski
GmbH
Heckelsberg 4
D-53773 Hennef
Germany

Borowski, Wiktor
Glasstudio Borowski
GmbH
Heckelsberg 4
D-53773 Hennef
Germany

Campbell, Marjorie
11 Inverleith Place Lane
Edinburgh
EH3 5QJ
U.K.

Coleman, Katharine
114 Winchcombe Street
Cheltenham
Glos.
GL52 2NW
U.K.

Conway, Jennifer
31 Oxford Road
Mistley
Manningtree
Essex
CO11 1BW
U.K.

Cribbs, KéKé
PO Box 1148
Freeland
Washington
98249
U.S.A.

David, Peter
Pinewood
Weare Gifford
Bideford
Devon
EX39 4QN
U.K.

Denison-Pender, James
Glenbrook House
Balerno
Midlothian
EH14 7BQ
U.K.

Dreiser, Peter
18 Rowland Avenue
Kenton
Harrow
HA3 9AF
U.K.

Dybka, Anne
Shop 19a Argyle Terrace
Playfair Street, The Rocks
Sydney
N.S.W. 2000
Australia

Eisch, Erwin
Glashütte Valentia Eisch
GmbH
94258 Frauenau
Germany

Eliades, Elly
Drossias – Stamatas 40a
Drossia
Attikis
Athens
Greece

Erlacher, Max
Erlacher Glass
26 West Market Street
Corning
NY 14830
U.S.A.

Ferguson, Cary
Ferguson's Cut Glass
Works
4292 Pearl Road
Cleveland
OH 44109
U.S.A.

Flavell, Ray
c/o The Crafts Council
44a Pentonville Road
London
N1 9HF
U.K.

Geissler M.B.E., Alison
52 Dudley Avenue
Edinburgh
EH6 4PN
U.K.

Gilliam, Tony
Little Reeds Studio
Andrews Lane
Ropley
Alresford, Hants.
SO24 0BZ
U.K.

Goodearl, Marilyn
Long Wood House
Kingswear
Dartmouth
Devon
TQ6 0DZ
U.K.

Gordon, Alasdair
23 Carrington Street
Palmyra
6157
W. Australia

Gordon, Kevin
3/1591 Nepean Highway
West Rosebud
Victoria
3940
Australia

Gordon, Rish
23 Carrington Street
Palmyra
6157
W. Australia

Harcuba, Jirí
Janouskova 1
16200 Prague 6
Czech Republic

Harris, Josephine
Studio 2
46-52 Church Road
Barnes
London
SW13 0DQ
U.K.

Henshaw, Clare
Forest Edge, Pipe Aston
Ludlow
Shropshire
SY8 2HG
U.K.

Höller, Franz X.
Ferdinand-Neumeier-Weg 4
D-94227 Zweisel
Germany

Hubert, Karin
Galerie Herrman
Poschinger Strasse 12
D-94256 Drachselsried
Bayer.Wald
Germany

Isphording, Anja
Am Weiher 19
34431 Marsberg
Germany

Jelínek, Vladimír
U Okrouhliku 2
150-00 Prague 5
Czech Republic

Kinnaird, Alison
Shillinghill
Temple
Midlothian
EH23 4SH
U.K.

Leibowitz, Edward
Jacob Jordaens 46
B-2018 Antwerp
Belgium

Lichtenstein, Bernd
Kolpingstrasse 21
D 28195 Bremen
Germany

Liddle, Isabelle
19 Tudor Crescent
Otford
Sevenoaks
Kent
TN14 5QS
U.K.

Mann, Denis
47 Dempster Street
Wick
Caithness
KW1 5QB
U.K.

Mannings, Gill
c/o Glass Dept. School
of Art & Design
University of
Wolverhampton
Molineux Street
WV1 1SB
U.K.

Mares, Jan
Blahoslavova 230
130 00 Prague 3
Czech Republic

Merker, Ursula
Haus Kynast
Gstaigkircherl 22
D-93309 Kelheim
Germany

Meyer, Deb
1737 Beaver Brook Lane
– Apt. A
Hunt Valley
Maryland 21030
U.S.A.

Newell, Steven
12 Victoria Terrace
London
N4 4DA
U.K.

De Obaldía, Isabel
Box 55-0070
Paitilla
Panamá City
Republic of Panamá

Palmer, Shirley
59 Burwell Road
Exning
Newmarket
Suffolk
CB8 7DU
U.K.

Peace M.B.E. F.S.A.,
David
Abbots End
Hemingford Abbots
Huntingdon
Cambs.
PE18 9AA
U.K.

Pennell, Ronald
c/o The Crafts Council
44a Pentonville Road
London
N1 9HF
U.K.

Procter, Stephen
The Australian National
University
Institute of the Arts
Canberra School of Art
Glass Workshop PO Box
804
A.C.T. 2601
Australia

Prytherch, David
11 Brook Road
Oldswinford
Stourbridge
West Midlands
DY8 1NQ
U.K.

Raynes Roberts, Mark
P.O. Box 21045
Orangeville
Ontario
L9W 4S7
Canada

Ruijterman, Jacques
Arundel Glass Studio
Tarrant Square
Arundel
West Sussex
BN18 9DZ
U.K.

Saare, Mare
Sostra 6-11
Tallinn
EE0006
Estonia

Sautner, Barry
123 Richardson Road
Lansdale
PA 19446
U.S.A.

Schluifer, Gernot
Klostergasse 8
A-6370 Kitzbühel
Austria

Schmidt, Christian
Auackerweg 5
94227 Rabenstein/Zwiesel
Germany

Scott, Sally
The Cottage
Cambalt Road
Putney
SW15 6EW
U.K.

Semecká, Lada
SK Neumanna 225
417-11 Teplice 5
Czech Republic

Sheppard, Tracey
10 King Alfred Place
Hyde
Winchester
Hants.
SO23 7DF
U.K.

Stevens, Mary
24 Manton Drive
Luton
Beds.
LU2 7DJ
U.K.

Takemasa, Takeo
74 East Fourth St.
Corning
N.Y. 14830
U.S.A.

Virgo, Hilary
67 Overstrand Mansions
Prince of Wales Drive
London
SW11 4EX
U.K.

Wenzel, Anne
Rotestrasse 22-24
D-24937
Flensburg
Germany

Whistler CBE, Laurence
Scriber's Cottage
High Street
Watlington
Oxford
OX9 5PY
U.K.

Whistler, Simon
Browns Cottage
Alton Barnes
Marlborough
Wilts.
SN8 4JZ
U.K.

Wolff, Prof. Ann
Transjö
S36052 Kosta
Sweden

Yamano, Hiroshi
3-10-1 Harumiya
Kanazu-cho
Sakaigun
Fukui-ken
Japan

GLOSSARY

Acid etching – see 'Techniques' section

Annealing – see 'Glassblowing' section

Bas-relief – literally, low relief (see **Relief engraving**) – in strict definition, where the carved figures or objects project less than one half of their true proportions from the background.

Blank – Any piece of glass which has not yet been engraved.

Burr – A small steel shaft, made to rotate at varying speeds, the end of which is coated with sharp diamond particles, carborundum or corundum. Available in a variety of shapes and sizes. Used extensively in drill engraving.

Cage cut – see **Diatreta**

Cameo engraving – a figure or design is engraved in relief on to glass cased with one or more layers of coloured glass and the under layers are cut away to provide a contrasting background.

Cased glass – glass with one or more coloured layers. As the engraver cuts through the layers, the different colours are revealed. Different shades can be achieved by a skilful control of the depth of cut. A typical example of cased glass is that of a disc – a clear roundel of glass has one or more coloured layers overlaid on to it.

Cast glass – The molten glass is poured into a mould to achieve the desired final shape for (if necessary) further working when cooled.

Copper wheel – see 'Techniques' section

Crystal – see **Lead crystal**

Diatreta – or **Cage Cut** – a complex and difficult technique in which features of a design (botanical, for example) are undercut so as to appear standing free of the main form, but are attached to it either by tiny concealed posts or by incorporating the points of attachment into the design itself.

Drill – see 'Techniques' section

Enamel – an opaque or transparent substance used as surface decoration, comprising a mixture of coloured pigments (from mineral oxides) and a flux, fired on to the glass at about 820°C.

Free-blown – a term used to describe glass blown without the use of a mould.

Flashed glass – see cased glass.

Flexible drive – see 'Techniques' section

Float glass – Architectural flat glass, available in various thicknesses. The molten glass is 'floated' – or poured – on to a bath of liquid tin, which gives an almost flawless finish. Float glass has a distinctive green tinge and is both hard (to engrave) and strong. This latter property is of obvious importance when one considers the considerable load which a large float glass architectural window or door, for example, has to withstand.

Gathered – the process in glass blowing where the blowing iron is dipped into the furnace to collect a blob (**gather**) of molten glass.

Graal – see 'Techniques' section

Intaglio engraving – where the design is engraved deeply into the glass, but appears to give the opposite effect, i.e. of standing proud of the background. The eye of a fish, for example, will be engraved as a circular concave depression, but when viewed from either side of the glass will appear convex.

Kiln casting – The engraver makes an exact clay replica of the piece of glass as it will finally appear. The clay model is then placed in a container and surrounded by a mixture of plaster and silica, which is allowed to dry out slowly. The model is then removed by carefully cutting the mould, and the remaining void is filled with small chunks of glass. The whole mould is then placed in the kiln for several days, and heated while the glass melts. After several further days of cooling and annealing, the mould can be removed from the kiln and broken away from the cast glass.

Lead crystal – 'Lead crystal' contains not less than 24% lead oxide. 'Full lead crystal' means that the glass contains not less than 30%.

Matt engraving – Where selected areas of glass are ground or etched to produce an opaque finish varying from a coarse grained texture to a fine white satin.

Microdrill – A small drill in which the electric motor is contained within the handpiece.

Mould-blown glass – the shape of the finished article is achieved by glass being blown inside a mould. The mould may be used simply to shape the glass or to impress patterns on to it. The mould may be the exact size required of the finished article, or part-sized, the glass being withdrawn to be further blown to full size.

Optical glass – Formulated for the manufacture of lenses etc. Glass which is harder than lead crystal and less suited to hand tools than electrically-driven types of working, but with its own particular brilliance.

Overlay – see Cased glass

Point engraving – see 'Techniques' section

Relief engraving – Where the background glass is removed to leave the design standing proud, as with a head on a coin.

Resist – see 'Techniques' section

Sandblasting – see 'Techniques' section

Slumped glass – This is a similar process to kiln casting. First of all the engraver's chosen shape is modelled in clay, covered with a plaster/silica mix as in kiln casting, and when fully dried out the clay model is removed, leaving the plaster cast to be used as a mould. However, the mould is not then filled with small pieces of glass as in kiln casting. Instead, a piece of flat glass is placed over the hollow mould and the whole placed in the kiln, where the glass sags or slumps slowly into the correct shape.

Stipple – see 'Techniques' section

Wheel engraving – see 'Techniques' section

BIBLIOGRAPHY

Dorigato, Attilia, and Klein, Dan, *International New Glass* (Arsenale Editrice, Venice, 1996)

Ebeltoft Glasmuseum, *Young Glass '97* (Ebeltoft, 1997)

Foulds, Diane E., *A Guide to Czech & Slovak Glass* (European Community Imports, Prague, 1995)

Guild of Glass Engravers – exhibition catalogues – *Jubilee Exhibition* (1977); *Glass Engraving Resurgent* (1979); *Festival of Engraved Glass '86* (1986); *Art on Glass* (1994)

Klein, Dan, *Glass – A Contemporary Art* (Collins, London, 1989)

Layton, Peter – *Glass Art.* (Black/Washington, 1996)

Matcham, Jonathan, and Dreiser, Peter, *The Techniques of Glass Engraving* (Batsford, London, 1982)
Mergl, Jan and Pánková, Lenka, *Moser 1857-1997* (Moser, Karlovy Vary, 1997)
Merker, Gernot H., *Glasgravur in Europa* (Bergbau- und Industriemuseum Ostbayern, 1994)

Newman, Harold, *An Illustrated Dictionary of Glass* (Thames & Hudson, London, 1977)
Norman, Barbara, *Glass Engraving* (David & Charles, Newton Abbot, 1981)

Palmer, Stuart and Shirley, *Glass Engraving Drill Techniques* (Batsford, London, 1990)
Peace, David, *Glass Engraving: Lettering and Design* (Batsford, London, 1985)

Whistler, Laurence, *Scenes and Signs on Glass* (The Cupid Press, London, 1985)
Whistler, Laurence, *The Image on the Glass* (John Murray, 1975)

INDEX

Aberdeen University, 118
Abergavenny, Church of Our Lady and St. Michael, 170
acid-etching, 19
Affolter, Konrad, 23-25
Africa, 50
Afzal, 125
Ainslie, Chris, 26-27
Alaska, Museum of Fine Arts, Robert O. Kinsey Collection, Anchorage, 164
Albuquerque Museum, 46
Aldgate, Church of St. Botolph, 143
Alexandria, 15
Altlussheim, 115
America's Cup Races, 79
Ampleforth, 172
Amsterdam, Kuhler Glass Gallerie, 118
Anderson, Nola, 148
Annan, Earl of, 118
annealing, 17
Antwerp, Jesode-Hatora-Beth-Jacob, 112
Appleyard, Tim, 154
Argentina, 118
Arsenal Football Club, 51
'Art in Action', Oxfordshire, 75
Artworkers Guild, 143
Arundel, 155
Ashburton, 149
Ashmolean Museum, 79, 187, 189
Australia, 40, 56-58, 79-87, 94, 106, 149
Austria, 64, 106, 126, 162-164, 180

Baden, Glass Studio Franzensbad, 149
Baden-Württemberg, 182
BAFPA, 147
Balerno, 51
Ballinluig, 118
Bank of England, 52
Barcelona, Centre del Vidre de, 126
BBC, 118, 172
beads, 15
Belfast, Royal Ulster Museum, 69, 94, 109, 137, 147
Belgium, 112
Bell, George, 58
Beloe, Robert, Trust Award, 68
Berchem, Gemeentelijke Academie voor Schone Kunsten, 112
Bergen, 79, 83, 86
    Brukskunst Forening, 79
Bergkuist, Knut, 20
Berkeley, Betty, 28
Berlin, Kunstgewerbemuseum, 60
Bern, 24
Birkhall, 172

Birmingham
    College of Art, 147
    School of Jewellery, 152
    University, 147
Blake, William, 39
Bloch, Martin, 58
Bohemia, 16
Bonn, 52
Bornholm glass school, 158
Borowsky Collection of Contemporary Glass, Philadelphia, 150
Borowski, Glasstudio, 29, 37
Borowski, Pawel, 29-31
Borowski, Stanislaw, 32-35
Borowski, Wiktor, 36-37
Bosch, Hieronymus, 34
Böttger, Gunnar,
Boyd, Guy, Studios, 58
Bratislava, 192
Brazil, 69
Bremen, 115
Breslau Art Academy, 34
Bridgetown, 83
Brisbane, Amanda, 147
Bristol, 26, 27
British Jewellers Association, 147, 152
British Museum, London, 147
Brno, Moravian Gallery, 106, 126
Broadfield House Glass Museum, Kingswinford, 69, 94, 137
Brock, Curt, 126-127
Bronfman, Charles and Andrea, 45-46
Brooklyn Museum of Contemporary Art, 112
Brorby, Severin, 79
Brunnier Gallery and Museum, Iowa, 150
Brussels
    Alliance Française de Belgique, 112
    Musées Royaux d'Art et de Historie, 106
    Pro Museo Judaico, 112
    Vlaamse Gemeenschap, 112
Buckfast Abbey, 26
Buckland Abbey, 26, 190
burr, 19-20

Cabot, John, 27
cage cut, 56
Caithness, North Lands Creative Glass, 118
California, 45
Cambridge
    Fitzwilliam Museum, 52, 187
    Kettle's Yard, 143
cameo engraving, 20, 22
Campbell, Marjorie, 38-39

Canada, 65, 69, 126, 152-153
Canberra, 149-150
    Australian National University, 94, 149
    School of Art, 149
Carlisle, 86
Carnegie-Mellon University, 136
Ceská-Lípa, 126
Charleroi, Musée du Verre, 112
Chef and Brewer, 141
Chelsea
    Christ Church, 190
    Flower Show, 79
Cheltenham, 40
Chingford, Church of St. Peter and St. Paul, 170
Church Commissioners, 52
Civil Aviation Authority, 172
Cleveland Museum of Art, 65
Coburg, Kunstsammlungen der Veste Coburg, 60, 69, 94, 112, 137, 150
Coesfeld, Ernsting Foundation, Alter Hof Herding, 165-167
Coker, Peter, 43
Colchester, 43
Coleman, Katharine, 40-41
Cologne, 15, 52
Colorado Springs, 46
Comford, Lady, 147
Company of Glass Sellers of London, 109
Compaq Computers, 118
Contemporary Applied Arts, London, 147
Contemporary Glass Society, 109
Conway, Jennifer, 42-43
Copenhagen, 94
Corning Museum of Glass, 24, 46, 52, 60, 65, 94, 106, 109, 112, 137, 143, 147, 150, 164, 167, 187, 189, 192
    New Glass Review, 147
Cornwall, 28
Corsica, 46
Covent Garden, The Glasshouse, 136
Coventry Cathedral, 18, 43, 118
Craft Consultative Committee, 109
Crafts Council, 109, 147, 150
    Bursary, 52, 149
    Collection, 69, 94, 127
Cribbs, KéKé, 44-46
Crieff, 86
cristallo, 15-16
Cronyn, Hugh, 43
Croydon College of Art, 166
Crystalex, Novy Bor, 69
    Branch Corporation, 126
Cumbria, 51
cut glass, 22

Czechoslovakia, 24, 69, 79, 88-89, 104-106, 126-129, 145, 147

Darmstadt, Hessisches Landesmuseum, 60
Dartington, 38
David, Peter, 47-49
Denison-Pender, James, 50-51
Denmark, 94, 112, 147, 150, 158
Devon, 149, 190
diamond engraving, 16
Donaldson, Grant, 85
Donne, John, 27
Drachselsried, Collection Herrmann, 60, 167
Dreiser, Peter, 21, 40, 52-55, 63
drill engraving, 19-20
Dudley, Glass Museum, 147
Duisberg, Carl, Scholarship, 180
Dunblane, 87
Dunkeld, Bishop of, 79
Düsseldorf
    Glasmuseum Hentrich, 94
    Kunstmuseum, 60, 106, 150
Dybka, Anne, 56-58
Dybka, Rudolph, 58
Dybka-Tichy Studio, 58

East Lothian, 51
Eastbury Church, near Lambourn, 187
Ebeltoft Glasmuseum, 112, 147, 150
Edinburgh, 71, 79
    Art Centre, 79
    College of Art, 38, 68, 71, 79, 86, 109, 118
    Festival, 118
    Heriot Watt University, 38
    Holyrood House, 72
    Royal Scottish Museum, 69, 109, 137, 150, 187
    University, 109
Egypt, 15
Eiff, Professor Wilhelm von, 19
Eisch, Erwin, 59
Eisch, Katharina, 165
Eliades, Elly Stai-, 18, 61-63
engraving techniques, 19-22
Erlacher, Max R., 64
Estonia, 156-158
etching, 19
Etruscans, the, 15
Eucla, Amber Hotel, 79
Exeter, Royal Albert Memorial Museum, 150
Exhibitions
    British Contemporary Crafts, Houston, Texas, 118
    Brno Triennale of Engraved Glass, 88
    Contemporary Scottish Glass, Glasgow, 118
    Eurodomus Turin, 106
    EXPO Brussels, 106

EXPO Montreal, 106
Festival of Engraved Glass, London, 118
Glaskunst/Glass Art '81 Exhibition, Kassel, 34
Glass '93, Japan, 147
International Contemporary Glass, Palazzo Ducale, Venice, 1996, 67
Jubilee Exhibition at Sandersons, 79
Kamenicky Senov Triennale, 126
Kanazawa International Glass Triennale, 106
La Défense, Paris, 87
Paris, 1925, 20
Scottish Glass Now, 118
Three European Craftsmen, 118
Venezia Aperto Vetro, 1996, 138, 147
World Glass Exhibition, 147
World Glass Now '94, 138, 147
XII Triennale, Milano, 106

Farnham, 149
Ferguson, Cary, 65-66
Ferguson's Cut Glass Works, 65
Ferranti, 79
Fitzwilliam Museum, 52, 187
Fladgate, Deborah, 39
Flavell, Ray, 67-69
Flensburg, 182
flexible drive, 19-20
Ford, Henry, Museum, 65
Forres, 109
France, 28, 34, 50, 126
Frankfurt am Main Museum für Kunsthandwerk, 60, 94, 106
Frauenau, 165
    Glasmuseum, 60, 94, 112, 147, 166, 167
Freed, Elaine, 18, 63
Freiburg, Augustiner Museum, 150
Fremantle, 83
    Bannister Street Craftworks, 79, 87
    City Council, 79
Friar, Ken, 51
Funtington, St Mary's Church, 190

Gate, 20
Gateshead, 150
Geissler, Alison, 70-72
Geissler, William, 71
Germany, 15-16, 24, 29, 34, 40, 59-60, 95-103, 106, 113-115, 130-132, 165-167, 182-184, 191-193
gilding, 15
Gilliam, Tony, 73-75
Glasgow
    Compass Gallery, 118
    Kelvin Hall, 81
    Kelvingrove Art Gallery, 109, 118
    Scottish Craft Centre, 87, 109
Glass Circle, 52
glassblowing, 15, 16-17, 20

Globe Theatre, 52-53
Gloucestershire, 40
Goldsmiths Hall, London, 147
Goodearl, Marilyn, 76-78
Gordon, Alasdair, 79-82, 83, 86
Gordon, Eileen, 83-87
Gordon, Harold, 109
Gordon, Kevin, 83-85
Gordon, Rish, 86-87
Gordon Studio, 87
graal, 20, 122, 126
Greece, 15, 61-63, 106
Groningen Museum, 60
Guild of Glass Engravers, 18, 63, 74, 75, 76, 79, 109, 141, 143, 155, 172, 185, 190
Gulf War, 39
Guttridge, Cliff,

Hadamar, Glasfachschule, 115, 133, 182
Hadelands
    Gallery, 147
    Glassworks, 79, 86
Haifa, Academy of Fine Arts, 112
Hald, 20
Hamburg
    Art Academie, 192
    Galerie L, 126
    Museum für Kunst und Gewerbe, 60, 94
Hampshire, 172
Hampstead, St. John's Church, 74
Harcuba, Jirí, 88-89, 138, 147
Harris, Josephine, 90-91
Harrach, 88
Harrachov, 88
Hawaii International Airport, 65
Hawke, Prime Minister Bob, 79, 87
Headington, Church of St. Andrew, 170
Henshaw, Clare, 92-94
Hereford College of Art, 94
Herefordshire, 147
Heriot Watt University, 68
Hergiswil, 24
    Glas Collection, 150
Hertogen Bosch, Glass Gallery, 126
Hessen, 115, 182
Hilden, 103
Hillier Trophy for Southern Britain in Bloom, 172
Holland, 15, 20, 26, 28, 106, 154-155, 185
Höller, Franz X., 95-97
Hubert, Karin, 98-100
Huntington Museum of Art, 134
Hutton, John, 18, 43
Hutton, Warwick, 43

Illinois State University, 149, 150
Immenhausen Glass Museum, 150, 167
Innsbruck, Tiroler Landesmuseum, 164
inlay, 15

intaglio, 22
Iowa, 150
Ireland, 46
Isle of Wight Glass, 85
Isleworth Polytechnic, 63
Isphording, Anja, 101-103
Israel, 112
Italy, 106
Ixelles, Musée d', 112

J. & B. Whisky, 79
Jacobite glass, 38
Japan, 40, 69, 106, 115, 126, 179-180,
   194-196
Jelínek, Vladímir, 104-106
Jerusalem, Bezalel Academy of Fine
   Arts, 112
Johannson, Willy, 79
Jutrem, Arne Jon, 79

Kaluga Glass Factory, 158
Kamenicky Senov
   Glass School, 106, 171
   International Engraving Symposium,
      69, 126, 147, 166, 171
   Museum of Glass, 147, 158, 167, 182
Kansas City Art Institute, 136
Karlovy Vary, 147, 171
Karlsruhe, Badisches Landesmuseum,
   94, 106
Kassel, 34
   Landesmuseum, 106
Katazawa Museum, 46
Kinnaird, Alison, 107-109
Kochrda, Josef, 126
Koganezaki Glass Museum, Japan, 147
Kolderup, Peter M., 79, 86
Köln, 60, 94
Kopecky, Vladimir, 103
Kosta Boda, Sweden, 192
Kosta glass, 20
Kramsach, 64, 164, 180
Kristallnacht-Projekt, Philadelphia, 88
Krosno, 29, 37
   Glass Factory, 34
Kuwait, 39
Kyoto, Museum of Modern Art, 137,
   150

La Jolla, James Copely Library, 46
Langan, Walter, 65
Laupen, 24
Lausanne, Musée des Arts Décoratifs,
   94, 150, 164
Lääne-Nigula Church, 158
lead crystal glass, 16
Leerdam glass, 47
Leibovitz, Edward, 110-112
Leicester
   Cathedral, 170
   Museum, 109
Leigh Yawkey Woodson Art Museum, 60

Lemberk Castle, 112, 147, 150
Leuven, Katholieke Universiteit, 112
Libensky, Professor Stanislav, 126
Lichtenstein, Bernd, 113-115
Liddle, Isabelle, 117-117
Liège, Musée du Verre, 60, 112
Lima, Peru, 76
Lincolnshire and Humberside Arts, 69
line engraving, 20
Liskeard, 28
lithophane, 166-167
Lobmeyr, J. & L., 60, 64, 147, 150
Lochen, Ida, 94
London, 51, 76
   Polytechnic, 58
Los Angeles County Museum of Art, 45
Lübeck, 192
Lucerne, 150
   Schweizerische Kreditanstalt Bank,
      150
Lviv Glass Museum, Ukraine, 158

McDonald, Alison – see Geissler, Alison
Mackenzie, Wilma, 38-39
McStay, Adrienne, 120
Madrid, Museo Municipal de Arte en
   vidrio Contemporáneo Ciudad de
   Alcarcón, 164
Malaysia, 69
Manchester, H.M.S., 147
Manchester School of Art, 140
Mann, Denis, 118-121
Mannings, Gillian, 122-125
Mares, Jan, 126-129, 138
Mastermind Trophy, 118
Matthew, The, 27
Mazda Cars, 118
Medek, Mikolás,
Meissen, 167
Melbourne National Gallery Art
   School, 58
Merker, Ursula, 130-132
Meyer, Deborah O., 133-134
Meyer, Jon, 134
Middle East, 74
Miller, General, 28
Millet, J.E., 50
Millville, Wheaton Museum, 134
Milwaukee, Marquette University
   Museum of Art, 167
Monro, Helen – see Turner, Helen
   Monro
Morley College, Lambeth, 40, 43, 52,
   63
Mornington Peninsula, Victoria, 85
mosaic, 15
Moser Collection, Karlovy Vary, 147
Moser Glass Factory, 126, 145, 171
Moutiers, 34
Munich, 192
   Academy of Fine Arts, 94
   Galerie für Angewandte Kunst, 94

Murano, 15
Murdoch University, 79
Mutitjulu Community, Northern
   Territories, Australia, 94

Nairobi, Kenya High School, 86
Nash, John, 43
Nathan, Michael,
National Arts Collection Fund, 51
National Association of Decorative and
   Fine Arts Society (N.A.D.F.A.S.), 51
National Trust, 190
N.B.C., 118
Neena, Burgstrom Mahler Museum, 134
Netherlands – see Holland
New Orleans Museum of Art, 167
New York
   Metropolitan Museum of Art, 106
   Museum of Applied Arts, 24
Newell, Steven, 135-137
Newfoundland, 27
Newick, St. Mary's Church, 170
News International Corporation,
   Australia, 150
Niederer, Roberto, 24
Nigeria, 118
Nordbruch, 122-124
Northern Arts/Sunderland Polytechnic,
   149
Norway, 79, 86, 147
Norwegian Royal Family, 79
Norwich, Castle Museum, 94, 137, 147
Notojima Glass Museum, Japan, 147
Nottingham Castle Museum, 147
Novy Bor
   Glass Technical School, 88, 126
   Symposium Collection, 112, 150
Nybro, Pukebergs Glasbruk, 192

Obaldía, Isabel De, 138-139
Oberhausen, Schluss, 60
O'Connor, John, 43
Öhrström, Edvin, 68
Okra Glass, 85
Old Chelsea Glassware, Melbourne, 58
Oldenburg, Landesmuseum, 60
Orrefors, 20, 68
Oscar de la Renta Perfume Company,
   Paris, 134
Oxford, 170
   Ashmolean Museum, 79, 187, 189
   Lincoln College, 170

Paddington, St. Mary's Hospital, 74
Palm Beach, Sammlung Lannan
   Foundation, 60
Palmer, Shirley, 140-141
Palmer, Stuart, 141
Palmyra, Western Australia, 87
Paris
   Ecole des Beaux Arts, 76
   Exhibition, 1925, 20

French National Collection of Contemporary Art, 147
La Défense, 87
Musée des Arts Décoratifs, 106
Passau, 94
Peace, David, 142-143, 170
Penland School, 46
Pennell, Ronald, 144-147, 152
Perth, Western Australia, 79, 83, 87
Perugino, Andrea, 26
Philadelphia, 88, 150
Museum of Art, 187
Pierrier, Kim, 83
Pilchuck
Collection, 147
Glass Center, 192
Glass School, 24, 46, 88, 126, 138, 147
Pilsen, National Bank, 126
Pliny, 15
point engraving, 20
Poland, 29-37
Polenovo, V. Polenov Museum, 158
Pollard, Donald, 64
Pope, His Holiness the, 79
Portland, Duke of, 118
Portsmouth, City Museum, 69, 137, 147
Prague
Academy/University of Applied Arts, 88, 103, 106, 126, 147, 171
Arts and Crafts High School, 88
Awards, 147
Kunstgewerbemuseum, 60, 106, 112, 147
National Bank, 126
Price, Charles, 51
Prizes
American Interfaith Institute Golden Award, 112
Bayerwald-Glaspreis, 166
Bayrischer Staatspreis Goldmedaille, 192
Central Swiss Glass Prize, 24
Coburger Glaspreis, 137, 192
Company of the Year Award, 118
Daniel Swarovski, 166
Ehrenpreis, International Glasart, Kassel, 192
Finn Lynggaard Prize, 147
Fragile Art International Glass Competition, San Diego, 147
George Kenner Award, 118
Glass Sellers', 109, 147
Kanazawa International Glass Prize, 147, 166
Kanazawa International Glass Triennale, 147
Kulturförderpreis, Ostbayern, 166
Lunningprize, 192
Nobel Prize, 118
Prix de la Sculpture en Verre, Liège, 112
Prijs van de Provincie Antwerpen voor Beeldhouwkunst, 112
Prijs voor artistieke roeping van het Ministerie van Vlaamse Cultuur als jonge glasbeeldhouwer, 112
Prijs voor glasraam van de burgemeester van Berchem, 112
Quadriennial of Medals, Kremnica, 88
Rakow Commission, 192
Regeneration Award for Architecture, 118
Sanford-Saltus Award, 88
Triennale of Engraved Glass, Brno, 88
Urkunde, Coburger Glaspreis, Coburg, 112
Worlds Crafts Council Glasprize, 192
Zentralschweitzer Glaspreis, 192
Procter, Stephen, 148-150
Professional Stained Glass Magazine, 65
Prytherch, David, 151

Qantas, 83

R.A.C., 79
Rabenstein, 166
Racine, Charles A. Wustum Museum of Fine Arts, 46
Ravenscroft, George, 16
Regensburg Museum, 60
Reigate Art School, 74
relief engraving, 22
Renton, Lord, 118
resist, 19
Rheinbach Glasfachschule, 52
Rhine, 15
Rhode Island School of Design, 138
Roberts, Mark Raynes, 152-153
Robinson, Mary, 118
Roche, 118
Rochester Institute of Technology, 88
Rogers, Howard, 64
Roman glass, 15
Ropley, 75
Rotter, Helmut, 24
Rotterdam, Museum Boymanns-van Beuningen, 60
Royal Academy of Music, 188
Royal Academy Schools, 166
Royal Albert Hall, 170
Royal Australasian Ornithologists Union, 87
Royal Brierley Crystal, 170
Royal College of Art, London, 94, 136, 149, 158, 178
Royal College of Physicians, 52
Royal Family, 74, 109
H.M. The Queen, 72, 79, 118, 187
H.M. The Queen Mother, 18, 118, 122, 172, 187
H.R.H. Prince Philip, 87
H.R.H. Princess Alexandra, 118
H.R.H. Princess Anne, 79
H.R.H. The Prince of Wales, 52
H.R.H. The Princess of Wales, 51
Royal Miniature Society, 52
Royal Society of Arts, 68
Ruijterman, Jacques, 154-155
Rumania, 110-112
Russia, 158

Saare, Mare, 156-158
Sackville, Owens Art Gallery, Mount Allison University, 112
Sadat, President, of Egypt, 134
St. James's Palace, Chapel Royal, 40
Salisbury Cathedral, 172
sandblasting, 20
Sandersons, 79
Sandle Manor School, Hampshire, 172
Sapporo, Hokkaido Museum of Modern Art, 46, 145, 147, 167
Sârs Poteries, Musée du Verre, 112
Sautner, Barry, 159-161
Schelling, Peter, 133
Schleswig-Holstein, 182
Schluifer, Gernot, 162-164
Schmidt, Christian, 165-167
Science Museum, 51
Scotland, 38, 51
Scottish Craft Centre, 72, 87, 109
Scottish Glass Society, 38
Scottish Society of Women Artists, 109
Scott, Sally, 166-170
Seattle, Pacific 1 St Center,
Semeckà, Lada, 171
Shakespeare, William, 52-53
Sheffield
Turner Glass Museum, 147, 170
University, 94
Sheppard, Tracey, 172-175
Shipley Art Gallery and Museum, 137, 150
Sidon, 15
Singapore, 126
Society of Botanical Artists, 52
Society of Designer-Craftsmen, 52, 190
soda glass, 15, 16
South America, 76
Southeastern Massachusetts University, 46
Spain, 106
Spencer, Stanley, 26
Spital Hengersberg, Kunstsammlung Ostbayern, 167
Stanwood – see Pilchuck
Steuben Glass, 64, 133, 180
Stevens, Mary, 176-178
Stevens, Sir Ninian, 79
Stipl, Karel, 88
stipple engraving, 20

Stourbridge College of Art, 178
Stowe, 188
Strathcarn Glass Co., Perthshire, 79, 81
Studio Glass Movement, 60
Stuttgart
    School of Applied Art, 19
    Württembergisches Landesmuseum,
        94, 167, 182
Sunday Times, 79
Sunderland Polytechnic, 149
Sussex, 155, 170, 190
Svarrer, Peter, 94
Swain School of Design, 46
Sweden, 40, 76, 79, 192
Switzerland, 23-25, 40, 106
Sydney, 58
Syria, 15

T.V.W. Channel 7, 79
Takemasa, Takeo, 179-180
Tallinn City Museum, 158
Tartu University, History Museum, 158
Tasmanian Glass, 85
Teachers Whisky, 79
techniques, 19-22
Theresienthal, Stadt Weiden
    Glasmuseum, 94
Thompson, J. Walter, 76
Thornton Heath, Church of St.
    Andrew, 170
Tichy, Vladamir, 58
Tirol, 64
    Landesmuseum, 164
Tokyo
    Ida Glass Factory, 180
    National Museum of Art, 69
Toledo, Ohio, 60. 94
Toronto, Raynes Crystal Collection,
    Orangeville, 152
Transjö-Hytta, Sweden, 192
Tucson, Arizona, 133

Turner, Helen Monro, 38, 72, 86, 109, 118

U. N. E. S. C. O. Paris, 106
U.S.A., 24, 40, 44-46, 64, 69, 76, 88,
    106, 115, 118, 133-134, 138-139,
    159-161, 180
    Embassy, 51
Ukraine, 158
Ulm, Hochschule für Gestaltung, 192
Ústí Nad Labem, Institute of Applied
    Arts, 171

Valencia
    Art Museum, 164
    Musée du Verre, 112
Vallien, Bertel, 118
Venetian glass, 15-16
Victoria, Australia, National Gallery of,
    150
Victoria and Albert Museum, 52, 69,
    94, 109, 118, 122, 134, 137, 143, 147,
    150, 170,187
Victorian glass, 38
Vienna, 64
    Glashaus Lobmeyr, 60, 64, 147, 150
    Ministerium für Kunst und Kultur,
        164
    Museum für angewandte Kunst, 60,
        106
Virgo, Hilary, 181
Vladimir region (Russia), Gus-
    Khrustalny Crystal Museum, 158

Wagga Wagga City Art Gallery, 150
Waldglas, 15
Wärff, Ann – *see* Wolff, Ann
Washington, 126
    Glass Gallery, 118
    Smithsonian Institution, 60
Watt, James, Society, 147
Wausau, Woodson Art Museum, 134

Wenzel, Anne, 182-184
Wertheim, Glass Museum, 60, 167, 182
Werner, Jakob, 24
Wessex Children's Hospice dovecot,
    172
West Dean College, 52
West Heath School, 51
West Surrey College of Art and Design,
    94, 149
Western Australia, University of, 79
Westerwald, 115
Westminster Abbey, 143, 170
Wheaton Village, Creative Glass
    Centre of America, 103
wheel engraving, 15, 21-22
Whistler, Simon, 188-190
Whistler, Laurence, 18, 20, 43, 51, 185-
    187, 189
Whitefriars Glass, 48, 80, 86
Whitehaven, Church of St. James, 170
Wilkin, Neil, 40-41, 52-55, 77
Wiltshire, Church of St. James the
    Great, 172
Wimbledon College of Art, 26
Winchester, 74, 172
Wolff, Ann, 191-193
Wollman, 20
Wolverhampton College of Art, 68
Woolworths, 118
Worms Museum, 182
Worshipful Company of Glass Sellers,
    40, 74

Yamano, Hiroshi, 194-196

Zimbabwe, 118
Zurich, Bellerive Museum, 60, 94, 106,
    150
Zwiesel, 96, 103, 166
    United stained glass factory, 115
    Waldmuseum, 167